Time to Enjoy
Your Blessings

Dianne Haynes Miley

CPH.
Concordia Publishing House

*This book is dedicated to
the glory of God. I thank Him
for all the blessings He has given me.*

*For my family—
Chip, Nick, and Melissa—
you are my blessings!*

*For my mom,
who blessed me with life
and a Christian upbringing.*

Copyright © 1999 Concordia Publishing House
3558 S. Jefferson Avenue, St. Louis, MO 63118-3968

Manufactured in the United States of America

Library of Congress Cataloging-in-Publication Data

Miley, Dianne Haynes, 1962–
    Time to enjoy your blessings / Dianne Haynes Miley.
      p.   cm.
    ISBN 0-570-05347-1
    1. Women—Religious life. 2. Women—Conduct of life. 3. Women—Time management. 4. Spiritual life. 5. Christian life.
    I. Title
    BV4527.M44   1999
248.8'43—dc21   98-45942
                                 CIP

1 2 3 4 5 6 7 8 9 10   08 07 06 05 04 03 02 01   00 99

Time to Enjoy
Your Blessings

Contents

Introduction

How to Make the Most of This Book

Time to Enjoy Your Blessings is maximized when you appreciate the basics of God and family—your true blessings. This book will help you set priorities and goals, simplify your life, and organize your schedule and home to give you more time for enjoyment.

Fill-in pages are included at the end of each chapter to record ways you can apply the principles to your life. Photocopy the pages to add to your daily planner. At the beginning of each year, make fresh copies and fill them out to fit your current circumstances. It will be encouraging to note the improvements you have made throughout the year.

A daily planner is crucial to the time-saving principles outlined here. Calendar pages in the back of the book can be photocopied and inserted into your own customized planner. This method allows you to add or subtract needed elements to your planner to suit your lifestyle. I encourage you to use colored paper to color-code your planner. Secure a ribbon marker to your planner's binding to mark your place.

The central theme of this book is to *enjoy*. These principles and methods are designed to enhance your enjoyment of life. Don't become stressed because you cannot carry them out perfectly. None of us achieve perfection; life does not allow it. Use these methods as a *guide* to grow closer to God, closer to family, and closer to where you'd like to be in life. Please don't allow the pursuit of these goals to become all consuming, thereby rob-bing you of the enjoyment you are hoping to experience. While results are important, methods of getting there are crucial to living the kind of life God intends for you.

Revel in the grace of God, celebrate His love, and delight in the blessings He has given you!

Dianne

1

Making Your Blessings Priorities

"Of all the commandments, which is
the most important?"
"The most important one," answered Jesus,
"is this: 'Hear, O Israel, the Lord our God,
the Lord is one. Love the Lord your God
with all your heart and with all your soul
and with all your mind and with all your
strength.' The second is this: 'Love your
neighbor as yourself.' There is no
commandment greater than these."
Mark 12:28–31

Define Blessings

Family, friends, health, home, career, religion … are
these your blessings? Are some of these areas stumbling
blocks to your happiness instead of blessings? First, let's
define what our blessings are, what we wish they were, or
feel they should be. The easiest way to do this is with a
pencil and paper. I have to assume that you are reading

this book because you want to make a difference in your life; therefore, it is an action-oriented book. At the end of this chapter, there is space to record your blessings. Please make a copy of the page to place in your daily planner. Get a pencil and jot down your blessings on that page. Please use pencil—you may wish to revise your list later.

Blessings—List what your blessings are: the people, places, or things that make you happiest.

Potential Blessings—Write down those people, places, or things in your life that you wish were blessings, but presently are not making you happy.

Wish List—Make a wish list of elements currently not a part of your life, but that you wish were. Keep these realistic—they will become your goals!

Evaluate Your List

God

Is God on the List?—Your list of blessings will become the basis for your priorities. Is God included on your list? Do you think of God as a blessing? God actually deserves the very top spot. He is, after all, our Creator and He sent His Son as our Redeemer. Here are more reasons to consider God a blessing:

God Listens—God hears our prayers and always listens. "When he cries out to Me, I will hear, for I am compassionate" (Exodus 22:27). What a blessing He can be to us, if only we *ask* Him! "Ask and you will receive, and your joy will be complete" (John 16:24). Does this mean if you ask to win the lottery, it will happen? Probably not. The last part of the verse says, "your joy will be complete." God knows that winning the lottery will not bring us complete joy. We only need to look at Hollywood or Wall Street to see that money cannot buy lasting happiness.

God Delights in Us—True, God punishes sin, and the overarching consequence of sin is death. However, God created us not to punish us, but to enjoy our company and to share His wonderful blessings with us. "The Lord your God is with you … He will take great delight in you, He will quiet you with His love, He will rejoice over you with singing" (Zephaniah 3:17).

God Lives by the Rules—Our fear of God comes out of respect for His awesome power. Did you fear your father as a child? I did, but only when I had done something wrong. I feared his anger and his punishment. My fear was based on a healthy dose of respect for authority and power, and for a man who loved me and always tried to do his best for me. The same applies to God: We avoid sin because it displeases our Lord, whom we love, and we are afraid to sin, for fear of the consequences that result from our actions. God lives by the rules, but rest assured that as our heavenly Father, He wants only what it best for us.

God Is a Refuge—The Psalmist writes, "Blessed is the man who takes refuge in Him" (Psalm 34:8b). When do we need refuge? When we have problems, of course. Children run to their parents when they have a problem. As God's children, we can run to Him when we have a problem, no matter how large or how small, how sinful or how embarrassing. "Come to Me, all you who are weary and burdened, and I will give you rest" (Matthew 11:28).

God Loves Us—God's power to save us from our sins is the blessing above all blessings. "For God so loved the world that He gave His one and only Son, that whoever believes in Him shall not perish but have eternal life" (John 3:16). God's Son Jesus died and rose again, conquering the power of sin and death. God, through Jesus, gave us life. *God loves us!*

Family

Make Family a Blessing—Look back at your list of blessings. What else did you include? Family? If your family is more of a "potential" blessing, then make it a major priority. Get it moved up in the standings! A good Christian psychologist or good Christian books can help you if the problems are severe. Family love and acceptance is a basic human need and it deserves your best effort to make improvements. Chances are, you may already know what needs to be done to make progress here. Give it prayerful consideration and remember this rule of thumb: *you can't change others, but you can change yourself.* Pray that difficult circumstances will change.

Marriage—If you are married, is your spouse a blessing? This is also a major priority, even before your other family members. Marriage is the foundation of the family; without a partner, there would be no children. Even if the children do not belong to both of you biologically, your marriage is the foundation of your blended family. Keep that foundation strong or the home will collapse. Children quickly see the priority you put upon your marriage. They would like to be top dog—it is their nature as sinful human beings. But it is not best for them to be at the top. The marriage must come first.

Children—Be responsible and reasonable. You know that you must tend to a hungry baby even when you are having an intimate conversation with your spouse. But a teenager who interrupts by demanding immediate grill service should be told to go it alone in the kitchen. Of course, you should feed your family—even if they are teenagers! But use discretion and do not allow the children to rule the family. Take charge, make the marriage relationship a priority, and then explain to your children why you must maintain a strong foundation in your family. Once again, there are many Christian resources on marriage and children.

Christian Friends

Where Can I Get Them?—Did friends show up on your list of blessings? I hope so. If not, find some. The best place I know to find good Christian friends is a Christian church. Once you attend and get involved in a church that you agree with biblically, be friendly with others and you will make friends.

Who Needs Friends Anyway?—Maybe you're one of those people who thinks you don't need friends. Maybe you've been hurt by so-called friends. Well, everyone needs at least a few good Christian friends, the type you can depend on when you need someone to listen, someone to understand, someone to help when no one else can. Who will care for your baby when there's a family funeral? Not family. Who can you talk to when you have a family problem? Sometimes you need someone with an outside point of view. If your family members are not Christians, you need Christian friends all the more. When your family is far away, or just not close to you, you need friends. Don't wait until a crisis arises and you *need* a friend; make friends now. Join a group or committee at your church and get to know people. And don't forget to *be* a friend as well.

Financial Blessings

Your financial blessings of money, home, cars, and other objects should be at the very bottom of your list. God sometimes blesses us financially; it is up to us to put material goods in their proper place. Don't equate godliness with financial blessings. The two *do not* go hand in hand.

God most often blesses us with what we *need*, not what we want. His ways are not the ways of this world. We are to be content with the blessings that are ours, trust God's infinite knowledge, and realize that He knows best, even when we do not understand His reasons. "Turn my eyes away from worthless things; preserve my life according to Your Word" (Psalm 119:37).

Other Blessings

What other blessings did you list? Career, health, hobbies, talents? All of these are personal blessings. We'll talk about what place they have on your list later.

Potential Blessings

They've Got Potential—Now take a close look at your potential blessings. Are any of them major influences like God, marriage, or family? Why are they only *potential* blessings? Think about why you may be unhappy with these aspects of your life and consider what changes *you* could make to improve upon these potential blessings. Remember the rule of thumb: you can't change others, but you can change yourself. Make these relationships the most important things in your life and you will begin to see some changes.

Wish List

Turning Dreams into Reality—Now examine your wish list. Consider what you can do to make some of these wishes become reality. Pray for the strength and guidance from God to take steps toward realizing these dreams. Pray for God's will in your life and be patient. Chapter 2 will help you understand how to determine God's will.

Now that we've covered our blessings, let's examine how to move potential blessings and our wish list up to be counted as true blessings. First of all, based on what you've just read, you may want to revise some items on your list. Then, by making priorities and setting goals, we will work on moving those potential blessings up and realizing some elements of our wish list.

Priorities of Joy

Jesus

J Is for Jesus—God's purpose for blessing us is to bring us joy. To have complete joy in your life, your priorities should be in this order: Jesus, Others, Yourself, or the acronym JOY. I have found from experience that having a close relationship with Jesus, our Savior, is the beginning of true happiness. If we put Jesus first in our lives, He will take care of all the other "stuff." "But seek first His kingdom and His righteousness, and all these things will be given to you as well" (Matthew 6:33).

Priorities for Jesus—Prayer, Bible study, worship, and living a life dedicated to Him make Jesus a priority in our lives. Jesus understands our limitations and does not expect us to neglect a sick child so we can attend worship or Bible study. But we *can* pray or sing praises while attending the child.

Others

O Is for Others—For our own good, and for a godly, purposeful life, we learn to serve. If we put others before ourselves—our loved ones, family, friends, church, and others who need us—we will learn to serve gladly. Mother Teresa lived in destitute surroundings in one of the poorest nations in the world, yet she was happy and fulfilled. Why? Because she took refuge in Jesus, and she willingly served others. She had a purpose and her life was full. God didn't make us to be self-serving gluttons: "You, my brothers, were called to be free. But do not use your freedom to indulge the sinful nature; rather, serve one another in love" (Galatians 5:13). Jesus came to serve; He calls us to do the same: "And whoever wants to be first must be your slave—just as the Son of Man did not come to be served, but to serve, and to give His life as a ransom for many" (Matthew 20:27–28).

Priorities for Others—Write the names of the people who are your priorities, and put them in order. This is where you get to customize your priorities for your life. Say, for example, your children are grown and on their own, but your bedridden mother lives with you. In this case, your mother would have priority over your children; she cannot care for herself and they can. If you have young children, and your mother is reasonably healthy, the children will, of course, come first. Remember not to play favorites, especially among children. That is not the purpose of this exercise. The purpose is to physically set down priorities in practical terms of where the most needs are, so you can concentrate your energies where they are needed most.

Use discretion and constantly reevaluate the situation day to day and minute to minute. Remember the teenager who interrupted your heart-to-heart talk with your spouse? If, instead of demanding food, he'd had blood gushing from a major head wound, then naturally he would have gained priority!

Your immediate family (those living in your household) should take priority over extended family, friends, and outside activities. How wonderful that our closest blessings are where God wants us to spend the most energy! This does not mean that your children will be damaged if they *occasionally* need to be patient while you attend the needs of others. They will suffer, however, if others consistently come before them, as will they suffer if they come before God. Balance is the key. Each family's needs are different. Know your own limitations and abide by them.

Yourself

Y Is for You—Being last on the list does not mean you don't exist at all. You are a priority; you simply need to keep yourself in place and remember not to think *only* of yourself. Jesus took time to eat, rest, and pray; He took care of His own needs so He could better serve others.

Priorities for Yourself—These include health (physical as well as mental and emotional), recreation, career, etc. Be good to yourself and take care of yourself as the temple of God. "Do you not know that your body is a temple of the Holy Spirit, who is in you, whom you have received from God?" (1 Corinthians 6:19). Don't let God's temple become a shambles or it cannot serve anyone. If your health suffers, you will be of little help to those who need you. If your family is dependent on your income, and your career flounders, you will not serve your family well. Your emotional state affects your family.

Record Your Priorities

Once these priorities are straight in your mind, it's helpful to put them down on paper. There is space at the end of this chapter to record your new priorities.

Things to Remember

You Can't Please Everyone—Putting others as priorities in your life does not mean you must always please others—we all know that is impossible! Please God, please your spouse, please your children, and please yourself. Do what you can to please others, but don't obsess about it! It's up to you to run your life. Yes, we must serve others but there is often a difference between serving and pleasing. Many people refuse to be happy no matter what you do, and it's not your fault. Remember your own priorities and goals. While it is commendable to try to please others, don't beat yourself up if it cannot be done. Don't allow miserable people to destroy your happiness.

Revise Occasionally—Life is constantly changing and rarely black or white, but we need guidelines to give us some sense of order. That's why we need to establish priorities and physically write them down. Occasionally, you will need to revise them to keep pace with changes in your life. Stay focused on these priorities to work toward your goals more effectively. Your goal will be to maximize your blessings!

Prayer—Pray! Ask God to guide you as you set your priorites. He will listen and He will answer.

Photocopy the following pages and add them to your daily planner.

Blessings crown the head of
the righteous. *Proverbs 10:6*

I Am Blessed

My Blessings—The elements of my life that make me
happiest.

_____

_____
_____
_____

My Potential Blessings—Elements of my life that
should be blessings, but are currently not making me
happy.

_____
_____
_____
_____

My Wish List—Blessings I wish for that are currently not
a part of my life.

_____
_____
_____
_____

Still others, like seed sown among thorns, hear the Word; but the worries of this life, the deceitfulness of wealth, and the desires for other things come in and choke the Word, making it unfruitful.

Others, like seed sown on good soil, hear the Word, accept it, and produce a crop—thirty, sixty or even a hundred times what was sown. *Mark 4:18–20*

Making My Blessings Priorities

Priorities for Jesus—Prayer, Bible study, worship, and living a life dedicated to Him. (List specifics below.)

_____

_____

_____

Priorities for Others—Family, friends, church, and others who need me. (List specifics below.)

_____

_____

_____

Priorities for You—Health, career, recreation, rest, and relaxation. (List specifics below.)

_____

_____

_____

Making God's Goals Our Goals

I press on toward the goal to win the prize
for which God has called me heavenward
in Christ Jesus. *Philippians 3:14*

Establishing the Ground Rules

All of this talk about God's blessings may seem quite irrelevant if your life is in shambles. Your life, your family, your friends, even God may seem more like burdens than blessings. Sometimes, problems in life can be an indication of a deeper problem with God. If this is the case, your first priority—your first goal—needs to be reestablishing a healthy relationship with God. In doing so, you will not only make peace with your Lord and Creator, you will also gain somewhat of an understanding of how He works in and blesses your life.

When restoring any relationship, whether earthly or divine, one of the first steps is forgiveness—asking for forgiveness when we have done something wrong, accepting that forgiveness when it is given to us, and then forgiving others for their wrongs toward us. We accept God's forgiveness to live in the freedom of His grace but we must acknowledge our sins before we can accept forgiveness for them. "Repent, then, and turn to God, so that your sins may be wiped out, that times of refreshing may come from the Lord" (Acts 3:19). We also ask God's help in offering our own forgiveness to God if we are angry with Him, for our own sakes. He does not willingly punish us. He only chastens and disciplines us when we go astray from His will. "My son, do not despise the LORD's discipline and do not resent His rebuke, because the LORD disciplines those He loves, as a father the son he delights in" (Proverbs 3:11–12).

Our eventual goal is to have a strong and trusting relationship with God so that His will becomes ours and His goals become ours. Forgiveness is the first step; the second is to understand how He works in our lives.

Trials

For Strength—The question most often asked by Christians and non-Christians alike is: Why? Why is this happening to me? Why does God allow this to happen? Why is life so bad? I don't have specific answers; no one does. But God allows trials in our lives to make us stronger and to pull us toward Himself. Sometimes He has to pull pretty hard! Sometimes He only wants to strengthen us in preparation for a task He needs us to fulfill. "Consider it pure joy, my brothers, whenever you face trials of many kinds, because you know that the testing of your faith develops perseverance. Perseverance must finish its work so that you may be mature and complete, not lacking anything" (James 1:2–4).

For Proof to the World—Going through trials does not necessarily mean that we have been disobedient.

Sometimes God uses us to be an example of the mighty power of His Holy Spirit in us. Look at Job. He was blameless, yet he went through tremendous suffering. Surely those trials made Job stronger, but God's main purpose was to prove His love for and control of His creation.

Our lives impact everyone around us, not only our family and friends, but people from our neighborhood, church, school, and community. God can use our example to encourage someone we may never meet. The world is impacted not only by what people say about us but by how others react to us. Maybe our example of grace under fire is needed by others, either to strengthen their faith or to bring them to faith. When we encourage one person, that person's life influences dozens of others, who influence dozens more, and so on. Just as God's plan for Job was much bigger than Job himself, God's plan for each one of His children is much bigger than the individual person.

For Reasons We Do Not Know—We do not know God's plan for our future or for others around us. It is not for us to judge or reason why. "No, we speak of God's secret wisdom, a wisdom that has been hidden and that God destined for our glory before time began" (1 Corinthians 2:7). God sees the big picture; we do not.

Let God Be God—God is not malicious—ever. His motives are always righteous, good, and pure, as are His plans for our lives. " 'For I know the plans I have for you,' declares the LORD, 'plans to prosper you and not to harm you, plans to give you hope and a future' " (Jeremiah 29:11).

Rest in the assurance that our perfect heavenly Father wishes only the best for us. Don't try to figure out the intricacies of His plan (the hows and whys). Let God be God and trust His almighty knowledge and power to care for us. "And we know that in all things God works for the good of those who love Him, who have been called according to His purpose" (Romans 8:28).

Look Toward the Light

Seek God's plan for your life when setting goals. Do you feel that you don't know which direction to take? Do you feel lost in this dark and scary world? God is the light of the world. Without His light, we don't know what we may bump into next. But if we turn to God and look toward His light, we can clearly see where we are headed. "For You have delivered me from death and my feet from stumbling, that I may walk before God in the light of life" (Psalm 56:13). It's when we look away that we have trouble seeing. And if we turn in the opposite direction, our own shadow blocks the light and we wander farther and farther into the darkness, stumbling, falling, and hurting ourselves and others.

All we have to do is turn around and look toward the light! God is that light; He will guide us and keep us from stumbling if we focus on Him. Of course we cannot literally *look* at God in our sinful state; but God gave us a reflection of Himself in His Word. Turning to the Bible—reading it, studying it, and praying to God for understanding and guidance—is how we *can* look at God's light. "Your Word is a lamp to my feet and a light for my path" (Psalm 119:105).

Seek God's Plan

Through prayer and Bible study, we can discern God's will for our lives and set our goals in accordance with His plan. God will reveal His will to us if we ask Him. The prophet Amos writes, "He who forms the mountains, creates the wind, and reveals His thoughts to man" (Amos 4:13). Daniel echoes Amos' thoughts: "He reveals deep and hidden things; He knows what lies in darkness, and light dwells with Him" (Daniel 2:22). The better we know God's Word, the easier it is to recognize whether our goals model His intentions.

Circumstances and opportunities often lead the way for God to bring about His plan. "In his heart a man plans his course, but the LORD determines his steps" (Proverbs 16:9). Through trial and error, prayer and Bible study, we can realize our natural God-given talents and abilities, strengthen our weaknesses, and learn to recognize God-given opportunities.

Use these questions as you work to recognize God's will:

1. *Is it biblical?* God will never ask you to do something contrary to His Word. Don't allow Satan to fool you. If you have any questions in your mind, there are probably good reasons for them. Look up the subject in a concordance. (Many Bibles have one in the back. If you don't have a concordance, it's a wise investment.) Read the Bible verses relating to your question. Consult your pastor or a trusted Christian friend, and pray continually for guidance.

2. *Is it my gifted area?* God uses the gifts He has given you. If you are a wonderful singer, chances are the choir would be God's place for you. However, there are no limits to God's wonderful plans. If you *love* to sing, but are not particularly good at it, sing anyway. God can still use your voice! As a matter of fact, He calls all believers to sing praises to Him. The key here is to use your gifted areas as guidelines for your ministry but never as limitations!

3. *Is God giving you an opportunity?* God has a way of placing us where He wants us. When we have to force our way to be where we want or do what we want, chances are good that it may not be God's will.

4. *Is it the right time?* I tried to write a book when my children were preschoolers. It was difficult to find the time to write, and I didn't have a computer. I tried to write at my sister's house, using her computer, but it just wasn't working out. Finally I gave up. It wasn't the right time. (And I later realized it wasn't even the right subject.) I had recognized my gift, but the opportunity and timing were not there.

5. *Am I afraid of God's will?* For years, I was afraid that if I sought God's will, it would be some type of full-time ministry (like being a missionary in some far-off place) that I would hate. Either that or I would have to give up things I liked or even loved. In some cases, they were sins I'd become attached to. In other cases, they were relationships with nonbelievers. In all cases, once I conceded that I'd better follow God's will, He didn't take away anything that I wasn't *much* happier without. I found out that God knows me better than I know myself—and guess what? *He wants me to be happy!*

I'm not saying that discerning God's will is always easy. I have gone through some tough times learning to follow God and I know there will be more of the same in my life. I still become sad or angry; I still have stressful times. But I am much more content now than I have ever been. In my innermost being, I know I can handle anything that comes my way because I have God. I also have peace. Many people don't understand how you can have peace in a bad situation, such as losing a loved one. That's why God's peace is called the peace that transcends all understanding: "And the peace of God, which transcends all understanding, will guard your hearts and your minds in Christ Jesus" (Philippians 4:7). No sinful habit, no relationship, no creature comforts can compare with the contentment this peace provides.

Trust and Obey

I no longer fear God's will for me. If God wanted me to go to the heart of Africa, I admit I would be apprehensive. I would study long and hard to confirm that it is *indeed* His will. But if I know He wants me there, I also know my soul will not be at peace until I follow His will. And I know He wants only the best for me. He will take care of me and I can look at the experience as a great adventure that God is planning for me. The essence of "letting go and letting God" is not only faith, but *trust*. "Trust in the LORD with all your heart and lean not on your own understanding; in all your ways acknowledge Him, and He will make your paths straight" (Proverbs 3:5–6).

Set Your Goals

Take some time to fill in page 29 with your short-term and long-term goals. To maximize and even increase your blessings, you must set goals, but you must think carefully about whether these goals model God's intentions for your life. Acknowledge and accept your limitations, then consider what must be done to reach your goals and let these objectives guide your steps. Stay focused on your priorities and goals when making day-to-day decisions.

For example, if one of your goals is to revive your marriage, you will not want to take a demanding job that will further distance you from your husband. Even when the marriage is strong, you must seriously consider whether a demanding job will ultimately draw you closer or farther from the goals you want to reach. However, it is possible that your current job puts stress on your marriage because you are unfulfilled, your income is too small, or your husband is jealous of someone you work with. In that case, maybe the demanding job would actually improve your marriage. Weigh all the factors of a major decision carefully and prayerfully. Remember to communicate with the loved ones who will be affected and get their feedback.

In all decisions, whether major or small, consider the resulting consequences. Maybe it isn't a new job; it's simply whether or not to work late on a particular day. Will your husband be understanding because money is really tight right now? Or, will he be upset because this is the first night in a week that you can spend together? Contemplate the ramifications of each action you take, and never underestimate the wonder of communication. Don't assume you know what your husband's response will be. Call him and ask!

Seek Guidance

Don't be afraid to seek guidance. Talk to someone who has achieved your goal or who specializes in the area. Don't be afraid to seek professional help. "Plans fail for lack of counsel, but with many advisers they succeed" (Proverbs 15:22). If you need a counselor, a doctor, an accountant, a business or financial adviser, or a minister, see one. If expense is a problem, ask if there are reduced rates or a budget plan. Often you can get the original consultation free. In the case of a counselor in particular, keep your Christian ideals in mind. If a Christian counselor is available, meet with him or her. If you cannot reach one, sift secular advice through the strainer of God's Word. Throw away the chaff and keep the wheat. Mention your Christian beliefs to your counselor and ask him or her to keep them in consideration. You may even be a witness to him or her.

As you think and pray about your goals, write them down. Photocopy the following page and add it to your daily planner. Review your goals often and adjust them as circumstances or needs change.

Let your eyes look straight ahead, fix your gaze directly before you. Make level paths for your feet and take only ways that are firm. Do not swerve to the right or to the left; keep your foot from evil. *Proverbs 4:25–27*

Setting Goals

Short-Term Goals (within one year):

_____

_____

_____

Steps Needed to Reach Goals:

_____

_____

_____

Long-Term Goals (after one year):

_____

_____

Steps Needed to Reach Goals:

_____

_____

_____

Enjoying the Journey

For I have learned to be content whatever
the circumstances. I know what it is to be in
need, and I know what it is to have plenty.
I have learned the secret of being content in
any and every situation, whether well fed or
hungry, whether living in plenty or in want.
I can do everything through Him who gives
me strength. *Philippians 4:11–13*

The apostle Paul spoke these words while he was in
prison. With God's help, we too can be happy in any situation. Even if our problems seem insurmountable and our
goals seem impossible, with God's help we can overcome
difficulties, surpass obstacles, and move confidently forward in our quest to live life more abundantly!

Take Steps Gradually

Start Small—Making lifestyle changes is never easy;
there's no quick fix. *Start small*. Take steps gradually to
simplify your life ... *and enjoy the journey*! Too often we

see our goals as where we want to be and we think we'll be happy when we reach them. In reality, most goals are never fully met. For instance, as Christians, our main goal is to become more Christlike. We will never fully reach that goal in this lifetime, but all our goals, including becoming more Christlike, will be met when we get to heaven.

Allow Mistakes—Don't fret your life away, always frustrated and never satisfied. Allow yourself learning time, and allow for mistakes—they'll happen! Often we can get a good laugh if we learn to see the humor in our mistakes. We all learn by trial and error. Don't beat yourself up; allow yourself time to improve. Remember that every limitation you have is an invitation by God to do for you what you cannot do for yourself. Ask for His help and guidance and He will surely give it to you.

Growth Is a Constant Process—Life should be a constant movement toward where you want to be. You can be content with each portion of that movement, knowing with each step you are farther ahead than you were before. It is important to remember, however, that getting a job, losing weight, cleaning a closet, or even buying a house is not permanent; each can easily be lost. If the taxes aren't paid, and the termites kept away, even the house will be lost. All must be constantly maintained, even while many other goals lurk on the horizon. (When one thing is achieved, we yearn for more; that is growth.)

Enjoy the Journey—But don't despair! *Enjoy the journey.* Life is too short to be miserable, and God doesn't wish it to be so. "A cheerful heart is good medicine, but a crushed spirit dries up the bones" (Proverbs 17:22). Life on this earth is never complete or perfect. About the time you get the garden all weeded, the weeds begin sprouting up again. That's life, as they say. Take enjoyment in the moment and be satisfied with today.

Contentment

Godliness—Remember, Paul was content in prison. How was that possible? Was he delirious? No. He had the Holy Spirit within him, as every Christian does. He knew that this life is temporary; he had the hope and courage given by God. "But godliness with contentment is great gain. For we brought nothing into the world, and we can take nothing out of it. But if we have food and clothing, we will be content with that" (1 Timothy 6:6–8).

Hope—" 'For I know the plans I have for you,' declares the LORD, 'plans to prosper you and not to harm you, plans to give you hope and a future' " (Jeremiah 29:11). Our future is in heaven! No matter what happens on this earth, every Christian has a secure future with God in heaven.

Trust God—Sometimes we get angry with God for the state of affairs in our life. God can handle our anger; He's big enough. He wants us to turn to Him and ask for His help. He wants us to realize that we can't control our lives—only He has control. Some of the most troubled people I've ever known are those who want control. They are troubled because it is impossible. God controls the universe and we submit to Him to be truly happy. Once control is relinquished to God, a burden is lifted from us that we could not bear ourselves. "Praise be to the Lord, to God our Savior, who daily bears our burdens" (Psalm 68:19). Because God only wants the best for us, we can trust Him to work out the details of our lives much better than we ever could with our limited knowledge and power.

Don't Worry—We don't need to worry; God promised to care for us. Jesus Himself tells us in Luke 12,

"Therefore I tell you, do not worry about your life, what you will eat; or about your body, what you will wear. Life is more than food, and the body more than clothes. Consider the ravens: They do not sow or reap, they have no storeroom or barn; yet God feeds them. And how much more valuable you are than birds! ... And do not set your heart on what you will eat or drink; do not worry about it. For the pagan world runs after all such things, and your Father knows that you need them. But seek His kingdom, and these things will be given to you as well." *Luke 12:22–24, 29–31*

God promises to provide for us!

Enjoy God's Blessings on Your Journey

True Blessings Are People

Make Time for People—In your quest for simplicity and organization, remember your true blessings are people. People are the one area that God does not intend for us to keep simple. Simplicity would be to keep the number of people you associate with down to a handful. Reality for most of us is a seemingly endless number of family, friends, coworkers, and acquaintances from childhood, high school, college, church, work, your children's school, neighbors, your parents' neighbors, your second cousins, and on into infinity. How can you just cut these people out of your life for the sake of simplicity? And if you could, would you really want to? The reason for keeping things simple is to have more time for people. Making time for them is the best way for us to be a blessing to God, to others, and to ourselves.

Family First—This is not to say that you should quit your job and visit friends all day; you need to be productive and provide for your family. Even if you are fortunate enough to be a full-time homemaker, you still need to put the needs of your household first. However, with an organized life, you will have time for both family and friends.

Visiting Friends—Take time to visit a friend but remember that she has a household to run too and possibly a job as well. Occasional short visits are more welcome than rare but extended ones (especially if unannounced). Do not wear out your welcome, or expect someone to spend inordinate amounts of time with you (whether you are visiting her home, she is visiting yours, or you have gone on an outing). Make yourself available, but do not be a nuisance.

When you visit, call first when feasible. Very close friends might appreciate a surprise visit, but always ask if they are busy before barging in for an hour or two. Maybe you can help with whatever they are doing, or maybe it would be best to visit another time. Visits can center around accomplishing something together—grocery shopping, Bible study, exercise, baking, or a project like painting or wallpapering (take turns helping one another). Or plan an outing: meet for lunch or take an afternoon to go shopping.

Remember your priorities of God, family, and then others. Take care of your own family first and allow your friends to do the same. Make your limitations known to others and appreciate theirs as well. Making time for people does not mean that you have to spend hours of idle time, although sometimes it's nice to just talk and sip tea! Weekends are perfect for that.

Weekends

Plan Some Fun—Weekends, ah, wonderful weekends. Make them special! Weekends are not just for catching up on work at home although they often seem that way! Weekends are for catching up on rest and relaxation, and catching up with loved ones. Realistically, I know there are jobs that must be done on the weekend. When possible, do those jobs as a family and make them more enjoyable. Adopt a leisurely pace; don't try to do too much in one day. Sleep in—you're allowed! Have a big family breakfast, then tackle housework, laundry, or yard work with renewed energy. Remember to plan some fun too. Chapter 8 lists some great ideas for having fun and enjoying the time you have together.

Take a Break—Keep one day of your weekend work-free. Attend worship with your family and enjoy the rest of the day together, relaxing or doing fun activities.

Financial Blessings

Enjoy God's Blessings—Don't feel guilty enjoying blessings from God. God does bless us with material things—money, food, clothing, housing, cars, etc. Don't be afraid to enjoy them. God blessed both Job and Solomon with great wealth. "God said to Solomon, 'Since this is your heart's desire and you have not asked for wealth, riches or honor, nor for the death of your enemies, and since you have not asked for a long life but for wisdom and knowledge to govern my people over whom I have made you king, therefore wisdom and knowledge will be given you. And I will also give you wealth, riches and honor, such as no king who was before you ever had and none after you will have" (2 Chronicles 1:11–12). God is happy to bless His people.

God's Share—It is not a sin to spend some money for enjoyment. I repeat: It is not a sin to spend *some* money for enjoyment. This is not permission to squander, waste, go into debt, be selfish, be greedy, or fail to tithe for the sake of your personal enjoyment. "Honor the Lord with your wealth, with the firstfruits of all your crops; then your barns will be filled to overflowing, and your vats will brim over with new wine" (Proverbs 3:9–10). It *is* permission to take pleasure in blessings from God, be they beautifying your home, taking a vacation, owning a boat, or collecting expensive trinkets (from jewelry to automobiles). That is, *if* we are giving God His share first, *if* we are generous and not hoarding our treasures selfishly, and *if* we can afford it without going into debt.

Debt—"Let no debt remain outstanding" (Romans 13:8). Debt is a necessary evil for *necessary* purchases— home, vehicle, and the like—that are too expensive to buy without borrowing. If you can purchase those items without debt, by all means do so. But be careful to pay others what you owe them and to give God His share.

Giving—God wants us not only to give, but to do so cheerfully and joyfully. "Each man should give what he has decided in his heart to give, not reluctantly or under compulsion, for God loves a cheerful giver" (2 Corinthians 9:7). This is to our advantage, for giving to both God and our fellow man brings joy to ourselves. Joy is in sharing! "The Lord Jesus Himself said, 'It is more blessed to give than to receive' " (Acts 20:35).

In All Things, Look for the Good

Once we are in tune with God's Spirit, we can learn to look for the good in all things and even make the best of bad situations. God can use even the worst circumstances to work out His will. As you look for the good, strive to see how you can grow stronger from trials. This is easier said than done, but it can be done. Nearly every situation has *some* good. Sometimes we need to see the benefits that another person receives, rather than focusing only on ourselves.

Good Out of Tragedy

I am well acquainted with tragedy. I have lost both my sister and my dad to cancer. My sister, Debbie, was only 29 years old, and her daughter was only 10 when Debbie died. How do you find good in this situation? It isn't easy. We have to think of Debbie—who is now in heaven—with no more pain *ever*, no more suffering. If we did not know she was in heaven, this situation would be much worse. My niece, Kim, has her father to care for her. If there had been a divorce, the situation would have been worse; if there had been more children or very young children, it would have been worse. Things could always be worse—even in a devastating tragedy like this. Keep your sanity by looking for the good and trusting God.

How will God use this tragedy for good? Well, I can't answer that—only God knows for sure. But I can see some clues if I look hard enough. All of our lives have been forever changed. Have we grown stronger? Closer to God? Debbie has, I have, my mother has, and ultimately, my father has.

My father did not handle my sister's death well at all. He began to have health problems almost immediately afterward. He was also extremely depressed. He grew very angry with God. His health continued to deteriorate until, three years after my sister's death, he was diagnosed with a brain tumor. He considered it his death sentence and indeed it was. My mom and I (and others) spoke to him about God and heaven. Previously, he had wanted to hear none of it; a mention of God would make him bristle with anger, sometimes fly into a rage. But now he would at least listen.

For five months we all dealt with his anger, his rapidly deteriorating abilities to function, prolonged hospital stays, and daily radiation treatments. He could not walk, go to the bathroom, or feed himself. He talked about suicide—often. He couldn't be left alone.

Finally, sometime during his last month, we began to notice a change in him, a change of attitude. Very gradually, the talk of suicide decreased. The anger subsided and was replaced by a sense of peace! Unfortunately, by then his thinking was so jumbled he often didn't make sense, and his speech was very difficult to understand. My father had to lose all control—over both mind and body—before he finally relinquished control to God. He had finally given up—given up his anger and his own will—given it over to God. It wasn't easy to recognize at first. And he never talked about it. At this point it was all he could do to make us understand that he needed a drink.

We continued talking to him—about God, heaven, and seeing Debbie again. He looked thoughtful. Sometimes he cried. One day, as I was leaving, I whispered, "I love you, Dad." No response. I began to turn away, then went back and whispered, "Jesus loves you." A huge smile spread over his face! This from the same man who five months ago flew into a rage if we mentioned God. He had changed! God had changed my father. Jesus was there! Had God brought good out of this tragedy? I think so! If my dad had died suddenly, I rather doubt he would have gone to heaven. Cancer gave him time.

Did my sister's death pave the way for my dad to trust in God? Maybe so. Having cancer made a drastic change in my sister's attitude toward God as well. Did her experience prepare my dad, make a change in him, that prompted his eventual response? I think so. How could it not? Debbie talked about God and heaven when she was ill. She was not a committed Christian before, so these were new subjects for her. Debbie was just as willful and stubborn as her father, yet she had turned to God. My father knew he could do it too. He had to; he also knew the alternative.

Do we still suffer the loss of my sister and my dad? Yes. My niece has no mother. My mom has no husband. My brother-in-law has no wife. My sister, brother, and I miss our sister and our dad. My children miss their grandpa and their aunt. But did these two tragedies turn out for the best? Under the circumstances, yes, I believe so. God did not put sin in our world—the sin that causes cancer, unhappiness, and all the curses of this earth; the sin that causes death. But God won the victory over the power of sin and death through His Son, Jesus Christ, and that victory is celebrated in heaven for all eternity. God brings good out of sin's evil, out of death comes *eternal* life. Heaven is definitely good.

Equipped with this knowledge, we need not fear death. If we do not fear death, what is there to fear? " 'Death has been swallowed up in victory. Where, O death, is your victory? Where, O death, is your sting?' " (1 Corinthians 15:54b–55). Our victory has been won. We can enjoy the journey—the journey toward heaven, the journey toward Christ.

How will you enjoy the journey? Photocopy the following page and add it to your daily planner. Pray about your journey every day.

I know there is nothing better for men than to be happy and do good while they live. That everyone may eat and drink, and find satisfaction in all his toil—this is the gift of God.
Ecclesiastes 3:12–13

Enjoying the Journey

Note the good things in your life at this time:

_____

_____

_____

_____

_____

_____

_____

How can you enjoy *today*?

_____

_____

_____

_____

_____

Think this way every day!

Simplify, Simplify, Simplify

Make it your ambition to lead a quiet life,
to mind your own business and to work
with your hands. *1 Thessalonians 4:11*

I'm still on the quest for a simple life; this book is only what I've learned so far. Much of it I'm still working on and trying to implement in my own life. The key to simplification is a back-to-basics attitude. Gain an appreciation for the plainer, simpler things, from good relationships to easy-to-clean decorating, easy-care hair, makeup, clothing, yard, house, etc. Don't get bogged down by a high maintenance lifestyle.

Simplification Requires Balance

Nothing is simple when your life is out of balance. Learn to balance your priorities, balance your commitments, and balance your schedule. Prioritize, but spread your time, energy, and money between God, family, friends, career, church, school, and whatever else your life involves.

Simplifying Your Relationship with God

Neglecting God—Many Christians, with the best intentions of putting God first, are so over committed to church activities that they actually neglect God; they don't have time to pray, read their Bible, or have family devotions. Church activities are good, but often those who *are* committed end up doing too much because so many others don't do anything.

The story of Mary and Martha is a perfect example of a lack of balance:

> As Jesus and His disciples were on their way, He came to a village where a woman named Martha opened her home to Him. She had a sister called Mary, who sat at the Lord's feet listening to what He said. But Martha was distracted by all the preparations that had to be made. She came to Him and asked, "Lord, don't you care that my sister has left me to do the work by myself? Tell her to help me!"
>
> "Martha, Martha," the Lord answered, "you are worried and upset about many things, but only one thing is needed. Mary has chosen what is better, and it will not be taken away from her." *Luke 10:38–42*

Martha was so busy working and preparing for Jesus that she was actually *ignoring* Him. Mary, on the other hand, sat at His feet and listened to what He said. Mary chose what is better. We can follow her example by spending time with God, reading His Word, praying, and worshiping. Of course, we should continue the work of His church as well, but not to the detriment of our relationship with Him.

God and Church Are Not the Same—While God and church are closely related, they are *not* the same. Being involved in lots of church activities does not necessarily mean you're involved with God. The only way to be involved with Him is to have a close relationship with Him and, like any relationship, this requires communication. Communication with God takes place through Bible study (listening to Him) and prayer (talking to Him). God speaks to us through His Word with the help of the Holy Spirit. This relationship has priority over church but to have balance, we need both. Do you have a balance in your life?

God instituted the church; it was His plan to establish a place where people can go to worship, to learn about God, and to encourage one another. No Christian is so spiritually mature that he or she does not need to learn and grow. Learning takes place by studying God's Word and by interaction with other Christians who have insights and experiences we do not have. Growth takes place through that learning experience as we become more like Christ.

Balance—If you are trying to grow in your relationship with the Lord, and you also need to be more active in church, join a Bible study or prayer group. This will help you achieve *balance*. Remember, start small. Add other activities when you feel God's calling and the time is right. Needs are everywhere. Ask God to help you recognize the right timing for the plans He has in mind for you. Then accept your calling and God's timetable.

Simplifying Your Relationships with Others

Communication vs. Activities—The same rules about God and church activities apply to family and friends. If you are so overburdened with activities such as sports, lessons, PTA, etc., that you don't have time to actually sit down with your family and talk to them, then you are missing true communication here as well. Remember, good relationships require good communication. You don't have to run around frantically and try to do it all; show your family love by being with them. Enjoy some of the fun ideas suggested in Chapter 8—Simple Pleasures. Remember to keep it casual and lighthearted. Go with the flow and let your family help decide what they'd like to do. Maybe just relaxing is all they want to do. Kick back and enjoy!

Quality Time Equals Communication—Quality time (whether with your children, your spouse, a friend, or with God) is time spent one-on-one with full attention to each other and with good communication. Play time is fine for young children. Older children, teens, your spouse, or a friend might appreciate a simple heart-to-heart talk. Try to learn what works best to help both of you open up and communicate.

Get Away—Sometimes an outing is a good time to be alone, away from home and other demands. And don't overlook the car as a good talking environment—no one can overhear you.

Try not to make elaborate plans, or you will miss the chance to converse. You may love shopping, but it is usually not conducive to great communication. Restaurants, parks, beaches, and hiking trails are good places to talk. Use your imagination.

When you're with your teens, visit a place where their peers don't go, possibly another town. This eliminates their potential embarrassment of being seen with their parents, as well as the possibility that they'll run into friends—and run off without you! It's wise to let them help you choose a destination where you can be together and talk. A disgruntled teen will not be in a communicative mood.

Listen Attentively—Once you get together, focus on the other person and give him or her your full attention. Talk openly and ask thoughtful questions. Listen carefully to the answers, and don't interrupt. Try to keep an open mind and not be judgmental—that stops communication cold. Be prepared to hear some things that may surprise or even scare you. Give yourself time to think them over and pray about it before responding. Treat your loved ones, including your children, with respect—the way you like to be treated.

Quality Christian Friends Are True Blessings

Friends who know the Lord help simplify your life. They encourage you in your walk with Him and support you in your journey toward becoming more Christlike. They help carry you and your burdens through good times and bad, and you can do the same for them. "If one falls down, his friend can help him up. But pity the man who falls and has no one to help him up!" (Ecclesiastes 4:10). If you do not have a friend like this, pray for one. He or she can make your life much more enjoyable.

Limitations

Limitations are critical when trying to achieve balance. A single mom who works until 5:00 cannot take her children to swimming lessons at 3:00. Don't worry about things you cannot change. Either take steps to change the circumstances (prayer is step one), or forget about it. Children need a contented mother more than they need swimming lessons.

Many limitations are much more subtle. Your body requires adequate rest, nutritious food, and plenty of water to function properly. While our bodies are very resilient and can handle some degree of abuse, consistent neglect of these basic needs pushes our bodies beyond their limitations. We end up stressed out, burned out, or stretched out (in bed, that is). Children are especially susceptible to stress as a result of insufficient rest. Not only do children require 8 to 12 hours of sleep per night, but they need time to relax and unwind and just *play*. Adults need this time too. Running hither and yon from 6:00 A.M. to 11:00 P.M. is not healthy. Accept the limitations of *your* body—everyone's is different—and respect those limits. Learn to recognize symptoms of stress in your family and make necessary changes to respect their limitations as well. Review the "stress relievers" at the end of the chapter and try to use them.

Career Options

We've looked at stressing ourselves *voluntarily* by over committing to activities. How much worse it becomes when the stress is imposed on us by others. Take work, for example. How do you change a stressful situation that you are required to endure in order to feed your family? First of all, seriously ask yourself: are you indeed *required* to endure this situation? Evaluate the following career options. Remind yourself there are options in every situation.

What If?—Play the "what if " game with yourself. What if you don't work overtime? Will you really be fired, or will you just have to curb your expenditures? What if you don't attend the office party? Will you really be demoted, or will your boss overlook an understandable absence, possibly not even notice? What's the worst that could happen? (It's usually not that bad and *never* the end of the world!) Then realize that "the worst that could happen" seldom happens.

Is Your Job Unbearable?—Often we endure hardships unnecessarily. If your job is truly unbearable, look for another job. Pray hard. Be willing to make a sacrifice for the sake of your sanity and your health. You may find that it's no sacrifice at all in the long run. Consider alternatives. Can you work from home, either with your current employer or another one? Can you start your own business from home? Be open minded and seek God's guidance. Change what you can and make the best of the rest. Keep your priorities in mind and continue working toward your goals.

Do You *Have* to Work?—Speaking of options, if you are married, do you *have* to work outside the home? Can you survive on one income? Many times extra expenses associated with employment cut deeply into your actual earnings. These include higher taxes by being in a higher tax bracket, child care, clothing, a second car, gasoline, parking, lunches out, and expensive convenience foods or fast food because you're too tired to cook. Even car insurance is more expensive when you drive more miles. Car maintenance is more too. Remember this advice: "Do not wear yourself out to get rich; have the wisdom to show restraint" (Proverbs 23:4).

Staying Home—By staying home, you can often save money. You have the time to cook from scratch, shop more carefully, and take care of things—from child care to housecleaning to home maintenance—yourself rather than hiring someone to do them.

Work Part Time—If quitting your job is out of the question, maybe working part time would be feasible. A part-time schedule allows you to bring home a paycheck and still spend a lot of time with your children. Many jobs offer flexible hours you could set around school or preschool schedules. A part-time job during your husband's off hours would allow dad to take care of the children. This saves money for sitters and lets dad share the responsibility for his children. Be careful not to over schedule these type of hours, however. You will lose touch with your husband if you never spend time together. This works best with children too young to attend preschool. Once the children are old enough for schooling, work for a schedule that allows the family maximum time together.

If You Must Work—If you must work outside the home, be very careful making other commitments. Time is precious—husbands are precious—children are precious. Consider your current circumstances temporary, for indeed they are. Realize that you need to make an investment of time in your children. This investment will pay off richly, far greater than any amount of money can offer.

Simplifying Suggestions for You and Your Home

While it is important to simplify the more abstract parts of our lives, perhaps the more immediate need is to simplify the "concrete" portions of our lives, to give us more time *now*.

Simple Beauty

Hair—Find a simple, classic hairstyle and stick with it for a while. Changing hairstyles constantly requires learning new styling techniques and possibly buying new styling tools. You don't want to be caught in a time warp, but a classic style should last at least two years and possibly up to five. Consider getting highlights rather than overall color or a perm. The highlights give your hair a body boost and don't need to be touched up as often as overall color. They are also less damaging to your hair.

Makeup—Use simple makeup techniques that can be done in five minutes or less. Find products and colors that work well for you and stick with them. Put your makeup on last, after eating breakfast, brushing your teeth, and getting dressed. This prevents messing up your makeup and doing it over.

Clothing—Purchase good quality, classic styles; think timeless and easy care. Find colors and styles that flatter you and stick with them. Forget fads. Choose items that will match pieces you already have, or buy pieces together. It's better to spend a little more and have an outfit you adore, than to save a few dollars and add another item to be shoved into the back of the closet. Buying from a catalog may sound simple, but it soon becomes a real hassle. You can't try things on or feel the fabric and when you add the cost of shipping and handling, the prices increase drastically. Find a store or two you can depend on for clothing you like, and frequent it. Treat yourself to a leisurely shopping trip when you truly need clothes. You'll save time and money in the long run. Always try clothes on. It takes less time than going back to make a return.

Even if you are a full-time mom, you need some nice, comfortable clothes that look good on you. Don't get caught in the trap of wearing dumpy clothes just because you're at home. When you look dumpy, you begin to feel dumpy. It's too easy to get depressed. Even an ordinary sweat suit can be jazzed up with a few colorful buttons sewn in a random pattern on the bodice, a piece of lace or ribbon around the collar, or a few ribbon roses. Fabric paints and iron-on transfers can also turn plain sweats into a cute outfit. If you're not crafty, add a cute necklace and earrings, or wear something with a collar underneath the sweatshirt to dress it up a bit.

Accessorize the wardrobe you have. Change the buttons for a new look. Buttons can also be sewn in a cluster to accent a collar. Mix and match your clothes for new combinations. Don't be afraid to wear a pretty sweater with a pair of stretch pants, or a nice blouse with jeans. You'll look and feel good. Style your hair and wear some makeup so you look your best. Even if it's just a ponytail and minimum makeup, you'll feel better if you're looking good.

Avoid anything that needs to be ironed, drycleaned, or hand washed unless it will be worn only occasionally, like a suit or party dress. Even many winter coats are machine washable. For those items you already own, many hand washables can be put through the regular wash cycle if placed in a large net laundry bag. Place items that need to dry flat on top of the dryer—it's flat and warm. Dress slacks and blouses can be smoothed on a flat surface and hung to dry, which eliminates most wrinkles. You can also hang lingerie, bathing suits, and anything spandex rather than put them through the dryer—it extends garment life dramatically. Put up a small clothesline in your basement by tying loops in the ends of thin rope and stringing it between two large nails on either side of the laundry room. In a more visible area, nice brass hooks could be used instead of nails. You can also string the clothesline above the tub and close the shower curtain. Outside, you can put up a temporary clothesline between two trees using the same method. When not in use, the clothesline can be removed.

Health

Basic Nutrition—Eat lots of fruits and vegetables. Eat balanced meals, including all the food groups. If you are a vegetarian or just don't eat a lot of meat, make sure to get enough protein from other sources. Drink plenty of water.

Vitamins—You can get most (if not all) of the vitamins you need from your diet if you eat healthy foods. However, if you're having a problem balancing your diet, you might want to consider vitamin supplements, especially vitamin C, any of the B's, and vitamin A. Check with your doctor to see what he or she recommends for you. Having all the necessary vitamins and nutrients will go a long way toward making you feel better, which, in turn, goes a long way toward simplifying your life!

Caffeine, nicotine, alcohol, and drugs—Many people rely on coffee in the morning but it has no nutritional value; try milk, which is good for your bones, or orange juice, which gives you an extra dose of vitamin C. The dangers of nicotine go without saying. Try not to use over-the-counter drugs unless you are ill, and even then, see if your doctor can recommend another course of action.

Exercise—Exercise doesn't have to be boring; you can get something done or have fun in the process. Housework and yard work are great examples, as are playing soccer with the kids, going for a walk, or splashing around in the pool. When you can't do these things, try to move around a bit and get your heart pumping for a while. Take the stairs. Park at the far end of the lot. Stretch.

Meal Preparation

Plan Ahead—Healthy, appetizing meals *can* be prepared in 30 minutes or less. Use basic ingredients and simple recipes. Appendix A offers several easy menu suggestions. Planning your meals for the week ahead saves you the time spent staring into the cupboards dumbfounded! It also prevents getting into the middle of a recipe only to find that you are missing an essential ingredient. Make out your menus and shopping list the day before your shopping trip. Check your cupboards for things that need to be used and figure them into your menu. Don't plan elaborate meals for every night of the week or you won't stick to your menu. Look at your plans for each day and figure meals accordingly.

Cleaning

Straighten up every day and your house will look clean even if it's not. Pick up clutter; enlist your family's help. This only takes a few minutes a day, and on cleaning day it's not so bad to vacuum and dust when you don't have piles of clutter to put away first. At least once a week, plan a few hours to take care of vacuuming, dusting, sweeping, and major cleaning of the bathroom and kitchen. The more you keep up with it during the week, the easier this chore will be. You'll find tips to help save time cleaning in chapter 5.

Decorating

Keep It Simple—Decorating should be unobtrusive and easy to clean. Things placed on the floor need to be moved and swept around, things on the walls, shelves, and tables need to be dusted. Keep it simple. For more decorating suggestions, see Appendix B.

Home Maintenance

Keep Up With It—Just like cleaning, if maintenance is done regularly, it's less likely to pile up on you. Take care of problems when you notice them and keep home maintenance simple. Recognize the value of a good handyman. If you aren't handy or just hate doing those jobs, hire someone to take care of them. It's cheaper in the long run to make the repairs a little at a time than to let small problems evolve into much bigger ones. A small hole in the siding is no big deal until insects burrow into it, set up house-keeping, and literally begin eating you out of house and home. Brick or vinyl siding is a worthwhile investment, as there is much less maintenance than on a stained or painted home.

Larger Isn't Always Better—Obviously, a small house is easier and cheaper to maintain than a large one. Before adding on or moving into a bigger house, consider how you could better use the space you have. This will not only simplify the work of maintaining your home, it will save you thousands of dollars as well. Chapter 6 will help with storage solutions.

Use Rooms Creatively—Tradition does not always work for every family. We recently moved many of our children's toys and large playthings into our unfinished basement. Now they have a place to make tents and play with cars and bounce balls and leave out half-finished puzzles. Their rooms are much cleaner and they can have more fun. If you have children who are young or the same gender but you do not have a basement, you could move all the children into one bedroom designated for sleeping and changing clothes, and turn the other bedroom into a playroom where toys are kept.

Bedrooms can actually serve many purposes besides sleeping. They can be a home office or computer room, a sewing or craft room, a workshop, an exercise room, a greenhouse with grow lights, a library or study, a family room, or even a dining room. They can be turned into a laundry room, an extra bathroom, or a bigger kitchen.

Consider All Your Options—If you have a porch, it can be used for many different purposes as well. A dining room can also be turned into a family room, office, play room, or the like. It can even be turned into a guest room either temporarily or permanently. If you want to turn room into a nontraditional place, but are concerned it will lower the value of your home, look into options that allow you to easily change it back to its traditional use. For example, you can create a wall with tall bookcases or tastefully done drapes. You can also put in a wall with large French doors and curtains; these open up the room, or close it off for privacy. French doors work whether you want to add a wall in an uncommon space or take out a wall that really should be there. Their versatility may even increase the value of your home.

Garages, attics, and basements can also be creatively used. A storage building or shed is a fairly inexpensive place to store the items you must move out when using these spaces as extra rooms. Not adding on to your home, or moving to a new home simplifies your life as well as your home maintenance.

Landscaping

Borders—A simple way to landscape is to put a border around something in your yard. These areas are hard to mow anyway and tend to need weeding. Around the house and other buildings, around trees, and around fences are also good places to landscape. Ask a nursery or landscape professional which plants require the least care.

Mulch—Mulching around your plants saves weeding and looks nice. It also protects your plants and keeps the soil moist. If you own a pickup truck, get a load of mulch ᴎ drive the truck to where you need the mulch. Unload ᵗly onto the area from the back of the truck. If you ᴎ a pickup, bagged mulch saves a lot of hassle for ᴎa cost. You can also buy a few bags at a time ᴎ and money. Having a dump truck unload ᴎh in your yard means you will be load-
ᴎmany wheelbarrows of mulch.

Ground Covers—Save yourself a lot of time with ground covers. You don't need to mow *or* mulch them. They are great for rocky areas or areas with stumps. Be careful with ivy if you don't want it to spread—it will grow right up trees or buildings. Ask your local nursery professional questions to determine what ground covers would best suit your location.

Plants—Invest in trees and bushes first; fill in with flowers later. Perennial flowers are the best bargains because they return bigger and better year after year. Many varieties bloom for very long seasons. Buy annuals for hanging planters and pots; invest in perennials for planting in beds. Many can be grown from seeds or bulbs. Learn about plants by borrowing library books or purchase a "plant encyclopedia" if you seriously want to learn more about gardening.

Location—Be sure to buy plants suitable for the location where you wish to plant them. This saves time and money, both now and later. Consult your plant encyclopedia, and if still unsure, ask a nursery professional. Don't plant trees or bushes too close to your home. They often grow larger than you think. Research the plant's "spread" to determine how large it will grow.

Accents—Use big rocks, driftwood, and antique items for garden ornaments. An old barrel cut in half makes two nice planters. Clay pots are cheap and can be painted or stenciled. Bird feeders, bird houses, bird baths, gazing balls, and sundials are also beautiful additions to your garden.

Pets

Simple Pets—Cats and fish are the simplest pets to own. They can be left home alone for a weekend and they don't need to be walked, let out, or bathed. Birds are beautiful and relatively simple to keep but they are noisy. Rabbits are wonderful pets. You can keep them outside in the summer and in the garage in the winter. Fill their pen with straw and it's good for a long time. Feed and water them, and hold them when you want to. Hamsters or gerbils are also low maintenance pets.

Dogs—Dogs are a lot of work. They provide great companionship, and it's said that they make you live longer. But they need to be fed, let out, walked, bathed, and given a lot of attention. You can't leave them home alone for more than a work day's time.

Plan ahead before getting a pet—know your schedule and the pet's needs as well as your finances. Food, vet bills, and boarding fees add up quickly.

Be Individual

God made you unique! Do what works for you and your family. Some things you will eliminate or scrimp on—things that don't matter much to you. Other things you will splurge on because you get so much enjoyment from them. This applies to everything from the brand of peanut butter you buy to the kind of house you live in, or the kind of vehicle you drive. Customize the ideas in this book to fit you, to fit what you enjoy and can afford. Only then will they truly simplify your life.

Stress Relievers

When there's no immediate answer to stress, try to relieve it by following some of these suggestions:

✓ **Remember the grace and forgiveness given to you through Christ's death and resurrection.**

✓ **Get up early enough to avoid rushing.**

- Eat a healthy, filling breakfast.

- Find time daily for solitude, prayer, and Bible study.

- Schedule a realistic day allowing buffer time for unforeseen problems, interruptions, and rest periods.

- Allow time for routine chores such as housework, laundry, and meal preparations.

- Use driving time to pray or listen to Christian speakers or music.

- Don't procrastinate! Do what needs to be done tomorrow *today*; do what needs to be done today *now*.

- Do unpleasant tasks first so they are behind you.

- Complete one major project before starting another.

- Write things down to help you remember.

- Make lists for shopping, errands, and jobs to be done.

- Use a daily planner.

- Slow down.

- Breathe deeply.

- Eat well 80 percent of the time. Stop eating *before* you're stuffed.

- Get a few minutes of exercise each day— more if you feel stressed.

- Get enough rest! Adults need 7–9 hours a night. Children need 8–12.

- Seek balance in all things.

- When waiting in line, meditate, pray, or start a conversation with a stranger.

- Keep a spare car key in your wallet and a house key hidden in your yard.

- Keep an extra $10 and a blank check hidden in your wallet.

- Save credit cards for emergencies.
- Make friends with people who don't have a tendency to worry.
- Learn to say no when you need to.
- Be content with what you have.
- Remember that everyone you see is carrying some kind of heavy burden.
- Do everything with love.
- Volunteer to help others.
- Think before you speak.
- Listen more and talk less.
- Be cheerful, especially when you don't feel like it.
- Be kind to the unkind—they need it most.
- Focus on loving rather than being loved.
- Hug someone who needs it.
- Laugh more!
- Live in the present.
- Don't worry about things you can't change.
- Give your burdens to God—He can handle them.
- Don't make promises you can't keep.
- Do nothing you'll be tempted to lie about.
- Delegate, and accept help without criticizing.
- Turn off the TV, phone, and pager for a little while.
- Take a relaxing shower or bath.
- Every day do at least one thing you really enjoy.
- Do your best at everything you do.

What specific things can you do to simplify your life?

Photocopy the following page and add it to your daily planner.

They devoted themselves to the apostles'
teaching and to fellowship, to the breaking
of bread and to prayer. *Acts 2:42*

Simplify, Simplify, Simplify

Ways I Can Simplify My Life:

_____
_____
_____
_____
_____
_____
_____
_____

_____
_____
_____

_____
_____
_____

_____
_____
_____

Organizing Your Life

For God is not a God of disorder but of
peace. *1 Corinthians 14:33*

Chaos results from either a lack of planning or too much commitment. Neither case is God's will for us. God planned the universe and everything in it with a sense of order. Failing to plan our days allows life to tumble on haphazardly until we suddenly realize nothing is being accomplished, and our lives are in chaos.

On the other end of the continuum, overextending ourselves causes us to lose the sense of peace that order promises. When we plan to do too many things, we inevitably don't have time to do them all. We certainly don't have time to pray or commune with God. We lose that inner sense of peace and life swirls about us, dragging us from one commitment to another. Our lives once more are in chaos.

The answer to chaos is balance. Plan your days so you can accomplish much, but don't plan so much that your schedule becomes burdensome. Allow time for prayer and Bible study. Allow time for unexpected interruptions or delays. Allow time for routine chores like housecleaning, meal preparation, and laundry. Allow time for worship, for family, and for rest. Allow time to enjoy your blessings!

First Things First

We Need God's Help—When I take time to ask God for help with this busy day, He helps! When I neglect Him because I have too much to do, He allows me to do it on my own. And what a mess I make! When I have a lot to accomplish, I don't have time to not ask for God's help! All it takes is a thought. When we take a few minutes to pray and read God's Word, He leads us. We actually get more done, do it better, and enjoy life much more than if we're rushing off without Him.

Slow Down and Get More Done—Try to eliminate "hurry" from your life. If we take our time, we make fewer mistakes. We think clearly and plan for contingencies that are forgotten in a rush. Those mistakes and contingencies often take more time to fix than it does to slow down and do the job properly the first time. Think of the man speeding to get to work on time. He was stopped by the police and received a ticket with a hefty fine. If he had slowed down, he would have gotten to work sooner and saved himself a good chunk of change and some humiliation as well. In addition to mistakes and oversights, rushing causes a sense of frantic unrest, panic, and even poor health, such as ulcers, high blood pressure, and the like. When we're sick, we don't accomplish much either. Slow down and get more done! Besides, it's a much more enjoyable pace of life.

Be On Time

Change the Clocks—If you're always late, set the clocks in your house ahead five minutes, and then forget you did so. If five minutes won't make a dent in your chronic tardiness, learn to allow yourself enough time (and a few minutes extra) to get ready. Getting ready includes more than getting dressed, doing your hair, and applying makeup. You also need to use the bathroom, gather up things to take with you, put on your shoes and coat, and physically walk to your car. Each of these things takes time—plan accordingly.

If you have children, this process becomes extremely complicated. You need to be sure the children are dressed, have hair combed and teeth brushed, have gathered things they need to take, have used the bathroom, have their coats and shoes on, then round them up again because the first ones ready have gone off to play (and quite possibly have removed their shoes and spilled something on themselves) while you were getting the last ones ready. What to do? Allow more time! Allow more time than you think humanly possible for getting ready to take. If you happen to be ready early, go for it! Leave the house—now—while you're ready! You never know what delays might be lurking out on the road.

Before you get out on the road, consider road and weather conditions. You may have to clean ice or snow off the car first, or your garage door may be frozen shut. You may have to shovel snow. You may need to let the car warm up because it is very cold outside. If it's hot, you may need to run the air conditioner to cool the car off to a tolerable level. Road conditions can be treacherous due to weather, traffic, or construction. There could be trains or school buses threatening to eat up a few more minutes of your time.

Many factors can gobble up time. No wonder you're late! And we haven't even considered the possibilities of a last-minute phone call, shoes tied in knots, or a car that won't start. Allow buffer time to absorb some of these delays. If you are typically 15 minutes late (figure out your own average), then allow 20 minutes longer than usual to get ready. This gives you a five minute buffer zone and that's not a lot; you may want to add more.

Don't wait until the last minute to leave the house. My own rule of thumb is to allow 10 minutes to "get in the car." (In the winter I allow 15 minutes.) If we need to be on the road at 8:00, I announce at 7:50, "Time to go!" This allows time to use the bathroom one last time, put on shoes and coats, gather needed articles, turn off the lights, lock the doors, walk out of the house, get into the car, buckle up, and start the car. (Ten minutes doesn't sound so unreasonable now, does it?) This is time people typically do not allow for. If they need to leave at 8:00, they begin this process at 8:00, which makes them actually leave 10 or 15 minutes late. They get frustrated and can't understand what happened; they thought they were leaving on time. This makes for frazzled nerves and unsafe driving.

Another common mistake is not allowing enough time for driving. If the trip usually takes 23 minutes, many people will round that off to 20. They are three minutes late before they start, without even considering delays along the way.

Once you arrive at your destination, you must park the car, load up your things again, gather the children, and walk into the building. It may be difficult to find a parking place, or it could be a long walk. You may have to wait for an elevator, or hang up your coats. Consider these possibilities when planning how much time to allow. I generally figure on being 10 minutes early. Sometimes I am early; very often I am only five minutes early, or I'm just on time.

Naturally, there will be times when you have allowed plenty of time but conditions beyond your control have still delayed you. Occasionally there will be an auto accident or a temporary road closing. People are understanding about these things, if it's not just one more excuse. If you are not usually late, it is understandable when something happens.

Attitude

My third-grade son, Nick, currently needs help with school work for about an hour after school. By the time we finish, I have to make dinner and set the table. After that I clean up the dishes and the kitchen, and pack lunches. The kids have to take their showers and get ready for bed, I tuck them in, then take my own shower. By this time it is close to 9:00 P.M. and I'm worn out.

I find myself resenting this time for school work. Previously, we spent only about 15 minutes on school work and then the kids would be out playing. This gave me 45–60 minutes I could spend writing, reading the mail, or whatever. I usually write in the afternoons, and it's always cut short when I have to pick up the kids from school. I'm anxious to get back to it for a few minutes before dinner and the evening rush. Now I can't do that, and it's been a struggle for me not to resent it.

When I do get back to my writing, I find myself saying "put your family before yourself." Ouch. Although I am doing so with my time, I'm not doing so with my attitude. Of course, it shows—I've been impatient and irritable. I apologized to Nick and we prayed about it together. Just acknowledging the problem has made it easier to deal with and God has helped, as He always does when we ask Him.

Remember, when your plans don't succeed—when your time instead is spent helping a child, or talking to a distraught friend on the phone, or whatever else came into your life that day—maybe it was God's plan for you. That may have been where God needed you most that day.

Routine

Routine is essential to time management. Be flexible but don't abandon your routine more often than you stick to it or it's not a routine at all! A "flexible routine" sounds contradicting, but it works! Allow buffer time for those weeks when you need to get a haircut, schedule a doctor's appointment, or take the car in for repair. Allow enough time for basic household duties such as cleaning, cooking, and laundry. Schedule realistic days and weeks that allow for interruptions, unexpected problems, and rest periods. Planning to get too much done in too short a time leaves you frustrated and disappointed. Unrestricted commitments quickly overtake your life, resulting in chaos. Acknowledging and accepting your limitations will ease your frustrations.

Figure out what works best for you, keeping in mind your own biological clock. Are you a morning or a night person? Periodically evaluate your routine and adjust it to accommodate changes in your life. Sometimes it may need a complete overhaul. The key is to be flexible with your routine.

Use a Daily Planner

If you are employed, planning is essential to keep track of all the things going on and all the things you need to do. If you're home full time, planning is equally important in order to get things done. It's easy to become undisciplined and get hooked on soap operas or sleeping late if you're not careful. Maybe you see these as the perks of your position; occasionally that's fine. The trouble is, occasionally all too often becomes more and more frequent, and before you know it, this has become a way of life. Avoid that trap by planning the jobs you wish to accomplish for the day and for the week. You'll not only get more done, you'll feel better about yourself.

Writing down goals and plans for the week makes you more likely to keep a schedule. When something comes up that threatens to deter your plans, it's easier to say no if the calendar is full for that day. You don't have to say that it's your cleaning day or family day; just saying, "I already have plans for that day" is enough. And you do. Of course you can be flexible too. If something comes up more important to you than your scheduled plans, the planner helps you remember what your commitments are so you can work everything in. One of the primary reasons for not over-committing yourself is that, inevitably, unexpected things will come up. Sometimes you must do them; other times you really want to do them. Be sure you remember your priorities when making plans. If you promised the children a day at the park, don't "bump them" just because a friend asks you to go shopping. It is important to keep your promises. Don't make commitments or promises you don't intend to keep.

Menu planning promotes balanced meals and makes shopping easier. It also prevents eating the fast food and pizza that threaten your budget and waistline. Money is saved at the grocery store if you plan your meals and stick to your list. When putting groceries away, clean out any old leftovers in the fridge. Move anything that needs to be eaten to the front. Assess canned goods and make a mental note of what you have. Move older items to the front, and try to use them in planning meals for the following week.

Scheduled days for shopping, cleaning, laundry, projects, etc. give the week a sense of order. Time is less likely to be frittered away if you have a plan for the day. Rather than being restrictive, a routine can be quite liberating; it gives you the freedom to do the things you really need and want to do. With a sense of order to the days and weeks, you won't feel frantic all the time or feel like time is robbed from you by things you have no control over. A schedule gives you permission to say no to those things that do not meet the criteria of your priorities.

Create a schedule that works for you. Use this sample schedule to get started—adjust it to fit your own needs:

Monday
Clean house

Tuesday
Laundry

Wednesday
Bible study, overflow

Thursday
Pay bills, file paper work, write letters, etc.

Friday
Plan meals for next week, make shopping list,
buy groceries, run errands

Saturday
Yard work, projects, play with the kids

Sunday
Church, visit family

Since most people are busy on the weekends, the house is usually messy by Monday. That's a good day to clean. If you aren't home much on weekends, or if you work full time and would rather clean on Saturday, do whatever works for you. You will still need to do daily straightening, pick ups and wipe ups, then do major cleaning on your cleaning day. Laundry usually piles up over the weekend as well, so I try Tuesday for laundry. On Wednesday I focus on a Bible study. The middle of the week is a good time for overflow work that hasn't been done yet. This also allows a buffer in case things come up on another day and you need to adjust your schedule.

Thursday is good for paying bills because most people get paid near the end of the week. Even if you don't get paid until Friday, you can still the write checks, and then mail them after you deposit the paycheck. Friday is good for shopping, also because of payday. Friday is one of the most popular, and therefore busiest, shopping days. Specifically for this reason, you may want to shop on Mondays and clean later in the week.

Try scheduling yard work for Saturday because it is often time-consuming and the family can do much of it together and enjoy the great outdoors. During the winter, Saturdays are good for projects such as cleaning out closets. Sunday is the Lord's Day—a good day to spend with family. Make Sunday a relaxing day off to rest up for the busy week ahead.

One major job per day is a good rule of thumb. Other daily responsibilities will take up the remainder of the day—don't worry! Trying to do major housecleaning, grocery shopping, and errands all in one day is just too much. If you pack all of that into Saturday, you need to give yourself a break. Try doing errands one day after work, or during your lunch hour. Try grocery shopping on Friday night. The housecleaning can be done Saturday morning and the rest of the day is free. If you like your morning free instead, clean in the afternoon. Your Saturday will be much more relaxed this way, and you'll have some time left for fun.

Special Projects—Projects include painting, wallpapering, cleaning closets, sorting recipes, sewing, crafts, planting a flower bed, filling photo albums, cleaning the basement, organizing cupboards, cleaning out files, doing the taxes, or anything else that is time intensive and does not fit into your ordinary day-to-day work. For someone who is employed full time, projects will usually have to wait for Saturday. However, many things can be done while relaxing in the evening—sewing, recipes, photo albums, and crafts for example. Writing cards or letters and catching up on reading can also be done in the evening. Try not to schedule more than one project per week. Wait until you finish the first project before starting another.

Schedule Time Off—Quite often, if you don't schedule a day off, if doesn't happen; it gets filled with chores, duties, and other work instead. Schedule at least one day a week off. Do something special—go the zoo or amusement park, get together with friends for dinner, or go to the beach. Put these days on your schedule. If budget is a concern, there are lots of inexpensive or even free ideas in chapter 8.

Full-Time Moms

Expectations—Sometimes it seems like working outside the home would be easier. Husbands, children, friends, and relatives expect so much of you when you are home full time. You are expected to be available to run errands for everyone, make various social commitments, help with sick relatives, babysit other people's children, and volunteer for unlimited activities at school and church, among other things. No one expects a "working" woman to do this much. After all, "she has to work."

Just Say No—The key to having the time to spend with those demanding little blessings of yours is to learn when to say no. Most full-time moms, however, not only have trouble saying no to numerous requests, but they play into this scenario by expecting too much of themselves as well. Determine the activities you can handle easily and do well. Stick to those. Reevaluate occasionally if you wish to change or add something new. If it's not feasible to add to your schedule, consider changing activities. Pray for guidance to find where God is leading you.

Perfectionism—Even in taking care of the family, homemakers often expect perfection: homemade everything from bread to soups to apple pies, a spotlessly clean home and perfectly groomed children, handmade clothing and home fashions, home-grown vegetables, fabulous holiday preparations, handcrafted gifts, elaborate meals and desserts. And they never miss a school, church, or community event. It's the Martha Stewart syndrome. Remind you of the Martha in Luke 10?

Priorities—There's nothing wrong with wanting to help others, and there's nothing wrong with being the best homemaker you can possibly be. These are, in fact, quite admirable qualities. However, we must remember the priorities set down in chapter 1. When perfectionism becomes so time-consuming that it has essentially become a priority, it's time to reevaluate. Remember that needs are everywhere and God does not expect you to serve every one of them. Learn to discern what God's plans are for you.

Working Moms

Expectations—While a stay-home mom's job is difficult, yours is also hard. You have the responsibility of your children and a career as well. When a child is sick, you have to take off work, send the child to school sick, or find someone who will care for a sick child. No matter what you do, there's guilt. You are being pulled in so many directions it's impossible to follow them all. The key to sanity is to remember what God expects of you. God did not create you to be a super hero; He created you for His glory. You cannot glorify Him if you are trying to fulfill expectations that He did not set. Pray for guidance and peace to fulfill *God's* expectations.

Just Say No—The dual responsibilities of a mom who works outside the home make keeping other commitments extremely difficult. Be careful not to overcommit yourself; you will become frustrated and often disappointed when something doesn't work out. Activities that strengthen relationships with God or your family are highly recommended; Bible studies and youth groups are perfect examples. Even then, adhere to your limitations to maintain a calm and orderly lifestyle. Keep your schedule as relaxed as possible.

Perfectionism—A full schedule often leaves little

room for perfectionism, yet so many of us attempt it. Once your life is simplified and organized, it's much easier to "perfect" the remaining elements of life because there are fewer of them. A standard of excellence is commendable but living within the limits of time requires that you lighten up on those things that are not top priorities. Gourmet meals may not be possible but we can have healthy and satisfying ones. A spotless home may not be an attainable goal but we can pick up clutter and keep things orderly. Learn to accept a little less than perfection.

Priorities—Remember those blessings you listed in chapter 1? Keep them in your mind. Strive to be more like Mary in Luke 10. She knew what was important—listening to her Lord. Martha was missing the blessing because she was busy preparing for the Lord. The truth is, He was already there! And He is already here in our lives too. "Be still and know that I am God" (Psalm 46:10). To enjoy the blessings in your life, be still and appreciate them.

Simplifying the Rest of Your Life

So you've taken care of the big things. How do you save time on routine chores so you really can have time to enjoy your blessings? Read on.

Laundry

Laundry piles up into never-ending mountains. You spend the day washing, drying, and folding until not one dirty scrap is left. And then your husband comes home and off comes the dirty shirt, the pants, the socks. On the floor they land. (If you're really lucky they might land in the hamper.) Laundry may not end, but you can minimize it.

Is it Dirty?—Think about it. You work in an office; you shower before work; you wear deodorant; you didn't sweat, you didn't get dirty, and you didn't spill anything on yourself today. Are your clothes really dirty? If they were "dry clean only," would you get them cleaned before wearing them again? No? So they aren't really dirty, are they? Shake them out and hang them in the closet to air out.

What about Towels?—You take a shower, your body is clean; you dry clean water off your clean body with a clean towel. Is that towel now dirty? Hang it on a hook or towel rack or over the shower curtain rod. Let it air dry and use it again. Put up several hooks behind the bathroom door for each person in your family.

Centralize Laundry—Is it possible to install a laundry chute in your home? Our main bathroom is directly above the basement laundry room. Houses are often built this way to centralize the plumbing. My husband cut a hole in the floor of the bathroom closet and installed a sturdy shelf directly below the hole (in the laundry room). I put a large sturdy clothes basket on the shelf. He built a wooden "chute" around the hole in the floor to prevent anyone from falling into it. We do not own a hamper; all dirty clothes are thrown down the chute and are deposited directly into the basket.

If there's no way to install a chute, use a hamper. One hamper in the main bathroom really centralizes the dirty clothes and eliminates the chore of going through every room in the house to collect laundry. If you have a closet or large cupboard in the bathroom, use a large clothes basket instead of a hamper. It's easier to use because there's no lid, and it's easier to carry and unload.

Sorting—Use three baskets: whites, darks, and colors, which prevents a lot of pink socks. It's pretty basic— put three clothes baskets on the floor, empty the chute basket, and sort the laundry into the three colors. The basket that gets full first is the first one to get washed. If you have room to put three baskets in your centralized laundry location, then you can let your family sort the laundry as they throw it in the baskets.

Fold and sort laundry as you pull it out of the dryer. This saves time shuffling it back and forth in baskets. The clothes are less likely to be wrinkled, and you'll be glad it's done!

Cleaning

Bathrooms—Keep cleaning products where you use them most. Keep toilet cleaner, a toilet brush, deodorizing spray, glass cleaner, and a roll of paper towels in every bathroom. You can mount paper towels inside a cupboard door or, if you don't have any cupboards, use a self-standing holder made for paper towels. Paper towels can be purchased in smaller sheets to eliminate waste. A large roll of paper towels lasts several months.

When you use the bathroom and notice the mirror is dirty, it only takes a few seconds to grab the cleaner and a paper towel and wipe it down. Don't put it off because you don't have an hour to clean the bathroom right now, just clean as you go. This haphazard cleaning actually keeps bathrooms cleaner.

Kitchen—Get a handle on dirty dishes by having a routine. For instance, every evening after dinner I rinse the dishes and put them in the dishwasher. After breakfast and lunch I do the same. If I won't be home at lunch time, I run the dishwasher after breakfast, even if it's not filled to capacity, because I know that after dinner the dishes will not all fit. (If I will be home for lunch, I run the dishwasher after lunch.) While I make dinner, I unload the clean dishes and it's ready for more dirty ones. I don't usually run the dishwasher in the evening because we take our showers then, and because we don't like the noise.

Wipe down the stove and counters when cleaning up the dishes, and clean the sink. Put away anything that doesn't belong on the counter and the kitchen is reasonably clean. On cleaning day, sweep the floor, spot clean, and clean up pet dishes.

Living Room/Family Room—Pick up clutter daily. The best way to eliminate clutter is to control it as it occurs. Once it gets out of control, the task is so daunting we avoid it. This, of course, only allows it to grow worse and worse. When you come across an item that is out of place, put it away. Paper is the biggest culprit; minimize the amount of paper in your house—limit the number of newspapers, catalogs, and magazines you receive. Toss junk mail as you receive it. Don't deal with the same paper over and over; handle it the first time. If it's a bill, file it in a "bills to be paid" folder. If it's reading material, put it in its designated spot. The papers will be where they belong and your house will be neater!

Enlist your family's help: if you put it down, you pick it up. Before going out to play, going to school or work, or going to bed, everyone should pick up after himself or herself. This keeps the rooms livable. Families aren't perfect, but this rule helps minimize the work left for you to do.

Bedrooms—Pick up clothes and other clutter daily. Make, or at least straighten, the bed daily. Kids' rooms are a sore point with most parents. Get the kids to clean as much as you can, but don't let it be a dividing issue in your family. On cleaning day, use the feather duster and vacuum. Make sure the kids have things picked up off the floor so you can vacuum. If they're old enough, they can vacuum their own rooms.

Heavier Cleaning—Once a month or so you'll need to clean better than just what's listed here. Use a duster on a pole to clean cobwebs from ceilings and walls. Move things off shelves and tabletops and use a soft cloth and furniture cleaner. Wipe down cupboard doors and wood-work. Mop the floors and wash the throw rugs. Vacuum really well, moving small furniture and using attachments to get into the corners.

Paperwork

Make the Time—Set aside a certain amount of time each week—perhaps even a whole day—to pay the bills, balance the checkbook, write cards and letters, file loose papers, clean up your desk, and take care of banking or going to the post office. If you have a home business, paperwork day is a necessity at least once a week, and can easily take the entire day. Allow for it, and you won't be perpetually behind.

Bills—When bills come in the mail, put them in a file folder marked "bills." You could also use a letter tray, bas-ket, bin, or whatever works for you. On your weekly paper-work day, go through the file and decide which ones need to be paid this week. Write the checks, file the receipts, and take care of any miscellaneous paperwork such as bal-ancing the checkbook.

Cards—Birthday and anniversary cards can be writ-ten out and addressed ahead of time, then marked with a small sticky note on the envelope noting the date to mail for timely arrival. Keep these in order by date in an outgoing mail basket near the calendar/planner that you check daily.

Meal Planning

Planning Ahead—Plan your meals for the week based on what you have on hand. Plan an easy meal (like hot-dogs) on a day when you'll be doing a major project such as painting; this helps avoid the temptation to order pizza if it's not in the budget. Keep frozen pizza on hand for those days that don't work out as planned. Making meals in the crockpot is also a great time saver.

What to Keep on Hand?—Anything you can't live without! Bread, milk, eggs, juice, cheese, lunch meat, mayonnaise, ketchup, and mustard. If nothing else, you can make a sandwich. Canned tuna comes in handy if you run out of lunch meat. Pasta, spaghetti sauce, and canned fruits and vegetables supply a meal in a pinch. In the freezer, keep hot-dogs, pizza, ground beef, bread, chopped onions and peppers, French fries, and vegetables.

Rules of Thumb—Main meals should include the four basic food groups: proteins, carbohydrates, fruits and vegetables, and dairy products. Proteins include meat, eggs, beans, and nuts; carbohydrates include grains, bread, pasta, rice, potatoes, and corn; fruits and vegetables include juices; dairy includes milk, cheese, sour cream, yogurt, pudding, and ice-cream. Menus that do not include dairy can be supplemented with a glass of milk, or other dairy products can be added to the meal.

Create menus that not only include the basic food groups, but also have some color. Serve a variety of colors on the plate for appetizing appeal. An all-beige meal such as chicken, mashed potatoes, corn, and applesauce is boring. Substitute peas for the corn, or cranberry sauce for the applesauce. The plate comes alive!

Leftovers

Quick Lunch—If only a small amount of food is left over, it makes a tasty lunch the next day.

Two for One—Some recipes easily provide a second meal. Roast beef, for example, can be simply turned into barbeque beef sandwiches for another day. If you plan these type of meals, however, be sure to set aside enough for the second meal.

Smorgasbord Night—Occasionally you'll need to have a "smorgasbord night," also known as "clean out the fridge night." Leftovers can make a delicious smorgasbord, can be used to create a whole new dish, or they can be food for fungus. What a waste of your hard work and money! You can't really schedule a smorgasbord night because you won't know when you're going to need one ahead of time—you never know for sure how many leftovers there will be. When you see the need to do this, you put off the planned meal for another day.

If your family is like most, they do not relish the idea of eating leftovers, so you'll need to doctor them up. Microwave that big bowl that's half full of macaroni and cheese, then spoon the food into a clean bowl that's the right size. Fill several bowls this way with a variety of foods to pick from. Voilà! … A smorgasbord! If there won't be enough to feed the whole family, fix a simple entree to go with all the extra side dishes.

Try to coordinate the foods. For example, say your leftovers are macaroni and cheese, mashed potatoes and gravy, pepper steak, and green beans. This doesn't sound bad, but say there's not really enough for the whole family. Prepare a simple meat dish like steak or chicken breasts that will go with all the items you're serving. If you have a really diverse variety, like chicken à la king, burritos, and spaghetti, you might want to fix a separate meal for each person, and let everyone decide what they'd like or draw straws. You can still add something simple if there's not enough food; give everyone a big salad, some fruit, and bread or rolls.

Presto Chango—Another option is "disguising" your leftovers as something new. Meat, pasta or rice, and vegetables can be turned into a delicious soup or casserole. A word of caution, however, leave out anything questionable. Better to throw out that one item than the whole pot. You can also prepare that item in your next meal. Plain pasta or rice is a nice addition to soup; just remember that cooked pasta should be added after the soup is hot, just to warm it. It doesn't need to cook again; if it does, it will turn to mush.

Leftover mashed potatoes and gravy can be turned into shepherd's pie. Ground beef from tacos or sloppy joes (with the seasonings) can turn into chili or a noodle casserole. Spaghetti sauce with meatballs can become meatball subs. Keep the spaghetti and the sauce separate if a lot is leftover—this gives you more options. Plain spaghetti or pasta can be turned into pasta salad if you add Italian dressing and chopped vegetables. Pasta with cheese or white sauce is an interesting side dish for chicken or seafood. Use your imagination and be creative. Variety is the spice of life, after all.

Using things up can be fun and festive. Raw vegetables can be added to a stir fry. Cooked vegetables can be added to rice or pasta side dishes to give color and pizzazz. You can create your own combinations of mixed vegetables as well. Apples, oranges, and grapes that no one has eaten are gobbled up quickly when made into fruit cups in pretty dishes, or added as a garnish on plates. Apples can be added to many meat dishes or desserts. Add them to pancakes or slice them on top of frozen waffles. Oranges can be squeezed for juice. Add an orange slice to the edge of glasses of juice or iced tea and your family will wonder what the occasion is. Grapes can also be added to chicken or tuna salad.

Overripe bananas are often a problem. Your heart says, "Make banana bread." But often your schedule screams, "No!" There are other options. Make banana splits. Cut banana slices and add to strawberries and yogurt, cereal, oatmeal, or instant pudding. If they're really overripe, throw them in the blender with other fruits or milk for a yummy fruit whip.

Use Your Freezer—Sometimes there is so much left

over that it's best to freeze it. You will better appreciate that Thanksgiving turkey after a hectic day in the middle of December than you will for a solid week at the end of November.

Shopping

Make a List—Making a list saves a great deal of time and money (as long as you stick to it!). As you plan your meals for the week, put the ingredients you need to buy directly on it and keep a running list someplace handy for things you run out of during the week. List things in the order they are in the store (produce first, frozen foods last, etc); so you can skip an aisle or section of the store. (See the shopping list in the daily planner, Appendix C, page 169.) Limiting your time in the grocery store will help you stick to the list.

Consolidate Trips—Try to consolidate your shopping and errands into one trip per week. It also helps save time if you do your shopping while you're already out, on your way home from work, or taking the kids to school. Avoid extra trips to the store and avoid "convenience" stores altogether—they have less selection and higher prices. Even if they are on the way, it still takes extra time and money to stop there. If you plan ahead, you won't be forced to use them.

Got Kids?—When my children were preschoolers, my mother-in-law wanted to spend some time with them. This gave me a few wonderful hours of freedom that I really appreciated. If you have preschoolers, work out a situation like this if at all possible. If Grandma is not available, find a friend who will trade off with you at least once a month—you take her children for a play day when she's out shopping, and she does the same for you. Husbands can also provide a needed respite from the kids. Or, occasionally pay a sitter just to have some time alone. Your sanity will be restored!

Errands

Make a Route—The same rules apply to errands as to shopping. If you have a day that you can dedicate to shopping and errands, by all means do so. Figure out a route so you can take care of all your errands without backtracking. Save the grocery store for last so your perishable items don't spoil in the car.

Leave Early—The earlier you go out, the less crowded the stores will be, which saves time as well as aggravation! Learn what time stores open so you can be an early bird. Figure store opening times into your route for the day; you can visit the early openers first, and save the others for last.

Reevaluate as Life Changes

How you organize time will, and should, change with the ebb and flow of your life. A mother of preschoolers will have a very different schedule than someone without children, an emptynester, or even someone whose children are in school. Jobs, health, family situations, and involvement in activities will vary at different stages of life, requiring modifications of your routine. As your life changes, remember to adjust your schedule accordingly. Don't rigidly expect everything to continue its course indefinitely. Remain flexible to accommodate the changes life hands you. There's one guarantee in this life—it will change.

Think about specific ways to organize your life based on the suggestions in this chapter. Photocopy the following page and add it to your daily planner. Write down your organized goals.

But the noble man makes noble plans,
and by noble deeds he stands. *Isaiah 32:8*

Organizing Your Life

Ways I Can Spend Time More Wisely:

_____

_____

_____

_____

_____

_____

_____

_____

_____

_____

_____

_____

_____

_____

Organizing Your Home

But everything should be done in a fitting
and orderly way. *1 Corinthians 14:40*

Storage, Retrieval, and Reduction

This chapter will give you practical tips and suggestions on where to store things, how to add storage spaces to your home, how to make the most of the ones you have, how to find things easily by organizing that space, and how to reduce the number of items you store by establishing limits.

Where to Begin?

One Room at a Time—Which room in your house needs organization the most? Start there. Get that room organized to the best of your ability, then move on to another room. Just like simplifying your life, don't expect organization to happen overnight. Take small steps and make improvements that get you closer to your goals. Realize that this is a lifelong process that will not have a clear end. Once organization is achieved, maintenance begins. Don't stress yourself out! Accept the fact that you will have lapses into disorganization from time to time. The idea is to improve and make those times shorter and fewer.

Three Trash Bags—For organizing and cleaning (especially closets!), try the three-trash-bag method. Each bag has a destination other than where you are cleaning. The first bag is the "Put Away" bag. Anything that belongs somewhere else in the house goes in this bag. The second bag is the "Give Away" bag. You can add these items to a "Give Away Box" (we'll talk about that later) when you're finished. The third bag is the "Throw Away" bag. Using this method prevents you from leaving the area every few seconds to go put something away, throw something away, or give something away. You stay right there until the job is done and are less likely to become distracted by traipsing around the house. Stay focused on the job at hand, and work at it until it is complete. Even with the best-laid plans and the best of intentions, disorder will creep up on you occasionally. Grab three trash bags and take control again!

A Place for Everything—Establish the most convenient place to store each item and keep the item in that place whenever it's not in use. When you're through using something, don't put it down, put it away! If your family needs to be trained in this habit, train them! Make some rules about putting things where they belong, and mete out penalties for nonconformists. To keep things fair and to encourage yourself to follow the rules, let penalties apply to mom and dad as well. Once your family gets used to it, they will love knowing where to find things without searching the whole house first.

Functional Storage—Organization is the key to functional storage. Many of these suggestions require products that help achieve organization by dividing space into units that hold specific items. Most products are inexpensive and some can be fashioned from materials on hand. Look around your area for a home improvement or home fashions store that carries a wide variety of organizational products for the home. Many discount stores even have a good selection of these items. Browse the store and get ideas; often you can come up with your own solutions just by observing what's available. Put your imagination in gear and think, "How could I achieve the same results using things I already have?"

Using Things Up—Do not buy more cleaning products, canned food, makeup, hair products, etc. until you have used up what you have or are in danger of running out before the next shopping trip. Do what stores do with their inventory and put the new products in back. Use the old ones first. This method saves money as well as space.

Quality over Quantity

Keep Only the Good Stuff—Every home has a set amount of storage space. Admittedly, some don't have enough. Quite often, however, we just have too much stuff, more than we need and more than we will ever use. If you haven't used something for more than a year, seriously question if you will ever use it. Answer yourself honestly and be ruthless if the answer is no; that item is taking up valuable storage space. Get rid of it.

Seldom-Used Items—Some things you do use but not very often. Items for specialty projects are one example, like a wallpaper pan. Before buying (and storing) these types of items, consider other options. If you know someone who has one, borrow it. If you have one, lend it. Chances are you won't both be wallpapering at the same time. Other, more expensive items, such as power tools or large equipment, can be rented. This saves both a substantial outlay of cash and valuable storage space. Sporting goods are another item that can often be rented. If you only go camping, bowling, skating, skiing, or golfing once in a while, rent the equipment rather than buying it and storing it. Quite often, seldom-used items are obsolete or ruined by the next time you need them due to inadequate storage. Rented equipment isn't always the best but at least you're only paying a few bucks for it, you don't have to lug it back and forth, and you don't have to store it. Besides, it's more acceptable to have ugly bowling shoes that are rented than to be the proud owner of them!

Practical Storage

Keep Like Things Together—This sounds like a no-brainer, yet some people keep toilet cleaner under the kitchen sink. Invest in a toilet brush and bottle of toilet cleaner for each bathroom. (This is not a large investment!) Keep it where you use it—in the bathroom. This also prevents running out; if you have more than one bathroom, there's another bottle in the house!

Convenient Storage—When needed items are convenient, you'll be more likely to do the job. Duplicate items such as pens, pencils, and scissors are fine if they help you stay organized. I have scissors at the kitchen phone area for coupons; in the silverware drawer for food packaging; on my desk for paperwork, on my husband's desk, and in each child's desk; in the bathroom for cutting bangs and my husband's beard; in the laundry room with my sewing things; and my husband has scissors in his tool box in the garage. That sounds ridiculous, doesn't it? But it's convenient. The key to being organized and getting things done is to put things where you need them.

Kitchen

Storage

Cupboards—Take a long look around your kitchen and determine whether the problem is not enough storage or just too much stuff. An average home needs at least three drawers—one for silverware, one for utensils, and one for dishtowels; at least four top cupboards—one each for glasses and cups, plates and bowls, serving bowls and platters, and spices and baking goods; and at least four bottom cupboards for pots and pans, plastic containers, bakeware and small appliances, and canned goods. If you have these basic requirements, you should be able to function once you reduce and reorganize. If you do not have this minimum of cupboard space or if you wish there were more, you have several options to choose from.

The Stove—Some stoves have a drawer in the bottom for extra storage; it's a good place to put bakeware. My mother used to store skillets in the oven because we lacked space. Just be sure to remove them before preheating!

Cabinets—A hutch or china cabinet offers storage for dishes and glasses; sometimes it even has drawers. If the budget is a problem, scour the classifieds, estate sales, or tag sales. Consider unfinished furniture that you paint or stain yourself, or laminates that you assemble. Keep an open mind in your search. Baker's racks are popular and inexpensive. Any shelving unit or bookcase can store not only cookbooks, but dishes, glasses, pots and pans, canisters of dry goods, tins of tea or cookies, or myriad things. Save large glass jars and decorate them with stenciling, or secure a square of cloth over the top with a rubber band, and tie pretty ribbon around it. These jars can be filled with flour, sugar, coffee, tea, pasta, rice, cookies, crackers, beans, and the like. Keep these pretty things on the open shelves and hide less attractive things in the cupboards.

An armoire or wardrobe can be turned into a pantry or displayed open like an old-fashioned pie safe. Add shelving and accent it with lace trim or drape cloth napkins over the edge at an angle. Keep pretty dishes, homemade canned goods, jars of dry goods, or crocks filled with utensils inside. An old dresser can be used as a buffet. Fill the drawers with utensils, dishtowels, foil and plastic wrap, tablecloths, and bakeware. Decorate the top with a gingham cloth and use pots of herbs as bookends for your cookbooks. Drape a lacy tablecloth over the top and display teapots, cups and saucers, or pretty serving dishes.

If your kitchen doesn't have space for any type of extra cabinet, can you put one nearby, perhaps in the dining room, hallway, laundry room, utility room, or even living room? If the cabinet is closed, no one has to know what's inside. It's fine to keep dishes or cookbooks on open shelves in the living room if they are tastefully displayed. Browse magazines for decorating ideas. Move things around for an arrangement that pleases the eye. Add plants, figurines, or candles to make it look less like kitchen stuff. If you're still at a loss, ask a friend who decorates well for suggestions.

Benches—A bench with storage inside is a wonderful place to keep pots and pans or bakeware. Tablecloths, blankets, linens, even potatoes and onions, or recyclables can also be stored here. One of these benches by the back door is a good place to keep shoes, umbrellas, lunch boxes, or backpacks.

Shelves—Decorative shelves on the wall are a good place to display pretty dishes, tins, baskets, and candles. The tins can be filled with anything from tea bags to nuts to chocolate chips. The baskets can hold spare change, matches, batteries, potted plants, birthday candles, or cake decorating supplies. If the shelves are placed high on the wall, no one will see what is in the baskets.

Above the Cupboards—In some homes, the area above the cupboards does not have a soffit. This is prime storage area for seldom-used or decorative items. Large platters, vases, or fancy dishes can be arranged tastefully and accented with silk plants or flowers. This is also a great place to store a collection of baskets, tins, birdhouses, glass bottles, old dishes, or teapots. Use your imagination. If you don't use your cookbooks very often, they can be stored here between bookends for neatness. Bookends can be anything from pretty rocks to old crocks. If you do have a soffit, it can be lined with narrow shelving or plate rails. You can also use metal plate holders to hang a collection of pretty plates or old dishes.

Stairway Space—Many houses have a basement stairway close to the kitchen. The back of the door and the walls along the stairway offer areas to put shelving. Plastic coated wire shelving units that fit on the back of a door can be purchased inexpensively and used to store canned goods. If the walls inside the stairwell are too narrow for shelving, try lining them with pegboard, and you can store pots and pans on one side and brooms and mops on the other. Is there a closet that utilizes the open area above the stairwell? If not, this is wasted space. A good handyman can build a closet himself. If you don't have a handyman available, get an estimate from a local carpenter. Many of them do side jobs for half the cost. Ask around for references.

Pantry—If you don't have a pantry, look for an unused corner where one could be built, or a closet that could be equipped with shelving and turned into one. If space is really tight, consider a triangular pantry in the corner, similar to a corner cupboard. Consult your handyman or carpenter.

Remodeling—If the budget allows, remodeling or replacing the cabinets is a worthwhile investment in your home and will be a great benefit. This option is still less expensive than adding on or buying a bigger home.

Organizing

Cupboards—Examine the inside of your cupboards for "dead space" and think of ways to use it. If your shelves are movable, move them to dimensions that better suit your needs. If you have fixed shelves, shelving racks can be purchased for plates and bowls to make them more accessible (rather than being stacked a foot high) and better use the available space. Cup hooks can be screwed into the bottom of shelves to make use of the space above the glasses. Lazy susans, single or double, can be used to store spices and cleaning supplies.

Cupboard doors can be outfitted with several gadgets to store things. Towel racks, paper towel holders, or racks for foil and plastic wrap can be attached inside a bottom door. Calendars or bulletin boards can be attached to the inside of a top door. Instructions on the Heimlich maneuver, CPR, safe storage of food, how to use spices, etc. can be taped to the inside of a door for easy reference. Lists of telephone numbers can be placed here if your kitchen has a phone.

For bottom cupboards, roll-out bins can be installed to retrieve items from the back more easily. Even without these, if you keep the smaller pots inside the larger pots, you can neatly fit a lot in the cupboard. Racks are also available to keep baking sheets standing and easily removable. Bins can be used to keep plastic containers from falling on the floor when the cupboard is opened. These are easy to slide out and look through without crawling into the cupboard to find what you need from the back. It's also easier to keep plastics neatly stacked when they're contained. Small wastebaskets can be used to store rolls of foil and plastic wrap compactly. For large cupboards or pantries, plastic stacking drawers can be purchased to store anything from recyclables to potatoes and onions to plasticware to lunch items.

Refrigerator—Make use of the bins. If they are less than full because you don't keep that many fruits and vegetables, use them to store buns, bread, meats, cheeses, yogurt, or small items that get lost in the refrigerator. If you might as well call the crisper "the rotter" because you forget what's in there, then use that bin for something less perishable such as cans of soda, juice boxes, or extra condiments.

Move your shelves to conform to your needs. A lazy susan helps keep small items handy in the fridge, especially if you're short on door space. The best rule for the fridge is to have a place for everything and keep everything in its place. This way you will be able to find what you need and you will know what you have—or need to buy.

Counters—Some items are handy to keep on counters: canisters, cookie jars, coffee pots, and toasters are a few. Don't crowd your counters, however. It takes up precious work space, and things kept out need to be cleaned more often. Try to keep your counter-top items sparse and as decorative as possible. Pretty canisters and cookie jars add spark to a kitchen; a stained coffee pot and crumb-covered toaster do not. If you aren't fortunate enough to have an appliance garage, consider adding one. In the meantime, try to keep the coffee pot and the toaster in a discreet area and keep them clean.

Telephone Area—Most kitchens have a telephone and the area around it tends to accumulate a lot of clutter. If you have space, a small desk or table is useful to take messages and store pens, paper, and telephone books. This can even be your paperwork area if there's room. This is also a good place for the infamous junk drawer. We all wish we didn't have one, but it's a necessary evil. It doesn't have to be a mess, however. Use small margarine tubs, plastic baskets from strawberries, or small cardboard boxes as drawer organizers. Silverware organizers or desk drawer organizers can also be used. This drawer is a good place to keep pens, pencils, notepads, rubber bands, paper clips, scissors, a calculator, markers, coupons, a screw-driver, thumbtacks, tape, and a small stapler. This is not a good place, however, to store every tool you own (unless there are only three).

If you don't have space for a desk or table by the phone, look for a wall-mounted unit that offers a writing surface and a small storage area. If you're handy, you could even design your own. If nothing else, attach a message board to the wall so at least you have a place to write things down.

Safety Equipment—Kitchens are a good place to store some safety equipment such as candles, in case of a blackout or bad weather. A fire extinguisher can be mounted inside a cupboard or pantry or inside a closet door near the kitchen. A flashlight and extra batteries should be kept nearby as well. Or purchase a flashlight that plugs into an outlet and is always ready and charged—there's no need for batteries.

Establishing Limits

When the cupboards are full, chances are you really don't need any more dishes or gadgets. If you really want to add something, get rid of something else first. Don't overstock your pantry or freezer, either. Use things up. It's fine to keep a good supply of food on hand, especially during bad weather; but don't keep so much that you don't even know what's in the back of the freezer. Use it or lose it. Even canned goods don't keep indefinitely. Remember to put newly purchased items in back, and use up the older things first. Always use up opened food before opening a new package.

Bathroom

Storage

Cabinets—First, determine if you have enough storage space in your bathroom for basic necessities. Is there a vanity below your sink? Are there any drawers? Do you have a closet in or near the bathroom? If these answers are yes, you simply need to organize those spaces. If the answers are no, then you'll need to add storage. Even in the smallest bathroom, there is space above the toilet and the sink. Buy a cabinet or shelving unit designed to fit above the toilet. Look for the largest unit with the most closed cabinets that will fit your space and that you can afford. A mirror is usually above the sink. If the mirror does not include storage, replace it with one that does.

Below the sink you really need a cabinet. If you simply can't afford to invest in a vanity, you have a few options. Velcro or double-sided tape can be run along the perimeter of the sink and a sink skirt (purchased or handmade) can be attached. Behind the skirt you can store a plastic bucket filled with cleaning supplies, packages of bathroom tissue, tub toys, and even a shelf to hold bins for toiletries.

If you don't like the idea of a sink skirt, a small hamper or lidded basket can be placed under the sink to hold cleaning supplies, feminine products, toiletries, and the like. A large basket with no lid can be covered with fabric with elastic sewn into the edges to keep it tight. The fabric can also be secured with ribbon, although it's more difficult to open and close. A lid can be fashioned from a piece of balsa wood and attached with hinges, leather straps or shoelaces, or rope. Bathroom tissue, tub toys, bars of soap, or pretty bath products can be stored in open baskets. Baskets can be decorated, if you wish, with ribbon, ruffled trim, silk vines, or dried flowers. Baskets can also be painted or stained to match your decor.

Other cabinet options are similar to the ones described for the kitchen. Keep an open mind. Almost any type of cabinet can be modified for bathroom use as well as any other room. Wall cabinets can be hung on any open wall. If floor space is available, consider benches, stools, or small tables as places to set things or store things. Don't forget the tops of cabinets. Pretty tins or lidded boxes can hold extra cotton balls, swabs, feminine products, toiletries, potpourri, and so forth.

Closets—If you have a linen closet near your bathroom, it can be used to store cleaning products, bath products, toiletries, and towels as well as linens.

Organizing

Vanity Cabinet—People usually keep cleaning products under the sink. If that's the only place you have, so be it. If your children are young, move all the cleaning products to the top shelf of the bathroom closet. Install a paper towel rack inside the closet for ease of cleaning. If you must keep your cleaning supplies in the vanity, keep paper towels there as well. Child-safe options for vanity storage would be towels, feminine products, or bathroom tissue.

Drawers—Shallow plastic baskets make good dividers for bathroom drawers. They can be used for: hairbrushes and combs, toothbrushes, toothpaste, dental floss, lip balm, makeup, facial products, contact lens supplies, nail polishes and tools, hair accessories, or shoe polish and shoelaces.

Cabinets and Closets—Adjust shelves to best suit your needs; add extra shelves if the existing ones are too far apart. Designate an area for each type of item. Remember, closets are good for just about anything from medicine, shaving supplies, cleaning supplies, and light bulbs to linens, a step stool, and a bucket of tub toys.

Open Shelves—Towels can be neatly folded or rolled and displayed on open shelves; bathroom tissue can be neatly stacked and stored here as well. Decorative baskets can be used to store makeup, hair products and accessories, bars of soap, or bath products. Lidded baskets or boxes, tins or ceramic jars can store feminine products, cotton balls, swabs, or medicines. Glass jars can be used for cotton balls and swabs. Gathered fabric or lace can cover a glass jar to store unsightly items. Ribbon or twine can be wrapped around glass jars and glued on. Large baskets on the bottom shelves can store cleaning supplies. Adjust the shelves so you can't see inside the basket.

Shower—Use a rack to hold shampoo, conditioner, and soaps. Some even have hooks for washcloths, back brushes, or bath puffs. If you don't want to hang it from the shower head, attach a sturdy self-stick hook to the opposite side of the shower and hang the rack there. This prevents bumping into the rack and prolongs soap life.

Counters—Keep counters open enough to be useful; liquid soap and a box of tissues are handy things to keep there. On ours, I also keep a cut glass jar filled with cotton balls and a decorative glass bottle filled with mouthwash. One decorative item is plenty for a bathroom counter; a flower arrangement or candle looks nice. The back of the toilet can also be used for a decorative item such as a basket filled with bath products (pretty yet practical).

Behind the Door—Install several large hooks behind the bathroom door for robes, clothes, and wet towels. Use heavy-duty anchors so they won't pull out of the wall. Be sure to put a couple of hooks down low where children can use them.

Establishing Limits

Products—Follow the same rules discussed earlier: use things up before buying more and limit items to the space available. Don't buy scads of makeup, hair and skin products, or cleaning supplies without first using what you have. If you're buying new products because you don't like the ones you have, throw the old ones away. If you don't like them, why are you keeping them? If they can be used by someone else sanitarily, go ahead and give them away. But don't shove them to the back of the cupboard!

Towels—Once the shelf for towels is full, you have enough towels. Try reusing them a few times if you keep running out before laundry day. (Either that, or do laundry more often.) When towels get ratty and need replacing, don't stuff them on the bottom of the pile and put the new ones on top. If they need to be replaced, replace them. Then use the ratty ones as rags for washing the car, drying the dog, or cleaning up messes.

Bedding—Sheets and blankets take up a lot of space. Two sets of percale sheets and two sets of flannel sheets for winter are plenty. When they need to be replaced, keep one white flat sheet for miscellaneous purposes, and retire the rest. They can be used to cover furniture while painting, make children's tents, or be cut up for rags. In any case, remove them from the linen closet and put them with the painting supplies, in the play area, or with the rags. Extra blankets are very useful and it's hard to say how many you should have. Determine how much space is available; they take up quite a bit of room as well. Keep one extra blanket for each bed in case of a power outage, and put an old blanket in each car for emergencies. Remember to consider overnight guests as well. (Hopefully there won't be a power outage during their stay!)

Bedrooms

Organized Storage

Closets—You can purchase closet organizing kits to better use the space available. Rotate clothes by season, keeping current season clothes in front and off-season clothes in back. Within these sections, keep similar clothes—slacks, shirts, skirts, blouses, and dresses—grouped together. This also aids in considering options for mix and match, rather than always wearing the same skirt and blouse combinations because they go together and hang next to each other in the closet.

Cardboard chests can be placed in a closet to store lightweight items such as lingerie, socks, and stockings. Shoe racks will help store more shoes in less space. Shoe boxes for shoes worn less frequently can be stored on the top shelf. Extra blankets can also be stored there if the linen closet has no room for them. Luggage can be stored on the floor, in the back. Nest suitcases inside one another to take up the least amount of space. Inside the smallest one, keep travel supplies such as shaving kits, small bottles, toiletry bags, and a travel alarm.

Dressers—Designate each drawer for certain items. Have a sock drawer, an underwear drawer, a drawer for tops, and a drawer for pants. Clean out the things you never wear and give them away. Keep one old outfit for painting—that's all. (How often do you paint, anyway?)

Rotate tops and pants to the front of the drawer seasonally, as with closets.

Armoires—These old-fashioned pieces have really come into their own. They can be used to store all kinds of clothing and accessories, and can even substitute for a closet. They are commonly used as entertainment centers as well and do the job beautifully.

Night Stands—A shelf or drawer here is a good place to keep books, pen and paper, or lotions. If you have extra space in your night stand, don't be afraid to use it for clothes if need be. Lingerie or stockings fit nicely in the small drawers.

Trunks or Cedar Chests—These are good places to store extra blankets, a wedding dress, off-season clothing, or memorabilia. Keep one at the end of the bed or use one as a table or night stand.

Under the Bed—Don't stuff things indiscriminately under the bed. Get some large shallow boxes to keep things in and plan what will be kept there. (These boxes can be purchased in discount stores if you cannot find suitable sizes.) Off-season clothing, your wedding dress, scrapbooks or mementos, gift items, or purses are a few things that come to mind. This is also a safe place for the leaf to the dining room table, or even storm windows if you have no other place available.

Establishing Limits

Clothing—When no more clothes fit in the closet or dresser, it's time to clean out. You can get rid of those clothes in the back, and you'll never miss them. By the time you fit into that old dress again, it'll be out of style and you'd probably treat yourself to a new one anyway.

Jewelry—Get a decent-sized jewelry box. When it's

full, start cleaning it out. (There's bound to be stuff in there you aren't wearing anymore.) Good jewelry makes nice heirlooms. Costume jewelry is fun for kids to play dress up (no pins, please). Give anything else to friends or charity.

Shoes and Purses—Determine how much space is available for shoes and purses, then decide how many shoes and purses you really need and actually use. To be practical, dress shoes in two dark colors and two light colors ought to be enough. A black dress bag and a white one should serve any purpose, along with your everyday purse.

Kids' Rooms

Organized Storage

Closets—Follow the same guidelines for clothing. Children's clothes are not as long as adult clothes, so there will be some extra space in the closet. Sturdy plastic crates can be stacked inside for toys. Don't install permanent shelving, because those clothes will be getting longer before you know it. Plastic drawer units can be purchased to store small items such as blocks, cars, doll clothes, or art supplies.

Dressers—We've covered clothing. The top of a child's dresser can be a place to keep grooming items, especially for teenage girls. This will save a lot of time in the bathroom! Provide a large mirror and two small lamps on either side for even lighting. Hair brushes, combs, hair spray, makeup, perfume, deodorant, and the like can all be used in the privacy of her room. Keep her supplied with needed items so she's not running off with yours. Install a full-length mirror on the back of the door or on the closet door. She'll be happier, and you'll be able to use the bathroom.

Bookcases—It's a good idea to have shelving for books and toys. These can be easily made from wooden planks and bricks or cement blocks. Paint the planks and bricks bright colors that match the child's room. Stack a plank, then bricks, then a plank, then bricks, then a plank. Be sure to use a plank on the bottom to keep it flat and sturdy. Instead of bricks, you could use large coffee cans filled with sand and painted or covered with colorful adhesive vinyl.

Desks—School-age children really need a desk to do homework; it's encouraging to have a quiet place of your own to work. A table can serve as a desk, and a stool or barrel can serve as a chair, if need be. A large desk can be made from two two-drawer file cabinets and a door without hardware. Dress up the desk with a colorful pencil cup made from a juice can covered in wrapping paper and sealed with clear adhesive vinyl. Fill the cup with brand new pencils, colorful markers, and pens. Stock the desk with scissors, tape, and paper. A bulletin board above the desk gives the child a place to keep spelling lists, homework assignments, and book report instructions, along with whatever his or her heart desires.

Under the Bed—Beware of "shove it under the bed" syndrome. Get large flat boxes to store designated items. Games and larger items such as race tracks, train sets, etc., can be stored here.

Establishing Limits

Clothing—At least twice a year you'll need to go through young children's clothes to determine what's too small or worn out. A good time to do this is in the spring when you're getting out warm-weather clothes, and in the fall, when you're getting out cold-weather clothes. In between times, whenever your child comes across an item that no longer fits, set it aside in a designated area to save for younger children, give to a friend with smaller children, give to charity, or sell in a garage sale. Older children's clothes may only need to be checked once a year, and before school starts is generally a good time to do that, to help decide what is needed for the new school year.

Toys—You'll also need to go through toys periodically to determine what your children have outgrown, and also to eliminate broken toys. You can do this in the spring and fall when you go through clothes, or you can do this after birthdays and Christmas, when new toys have dulled the luster of the old ones.

Artwork/School Papers—Determine how much room you have to store papers. A bulletin board allows you to showcase artwork temporarily. When new art is made, the old can be tossed. Exemplary art can be saved in a designated box for artwork, special school papers, report cards, etc. Decorate the box by covering it with gift wrap, adhesive paper, or comics. You may also cover it with newspaper and use colorful markers to write the child's name in the headlines. This box can be kept in the top of your child's closet.

Limit what is kept to a handful of papers per school year, and keep them in chronological order. The easiest way is to put most recent ones on the top of the box, and write dates on the back. If you are truly ambitious, these can be placed in a scrapbook. For most of us, however, just getting them into a box in an organized fashion is an accomplishment. Keep this system down to one box per child. If you don't have space for a box, there are books available that have pockets and fill-in pages for each school grade. The book will only hold a few papers and maybe that's good! You can also design your own using a notebook or scrapbook if you have the time. When your children grow up, you can pass their box or book on to them. Your grandchildren will be quite entertained with it someday!

Living Room/Family Room

Organized Storage

Entertainment Center—These useful storage units hold TVs, VCRs, stereo equipment, videos, games, CDs, and tapes beautifully. Traditional entertainment centers and armoires can be used, as well as any large bookcase or shelving unit. If none of these are available, consider a table for the TV with a long tablecloth draped over it to hide other equipment stored below. If space permits, photo albums or old yearbooks can also be stored here.

Bookcases—A lot of things can be stored here besides books! Try to keep open shelving attractive. Framed photographs, a collection of candlesticks, figurines, silk plants, or handsome bookends can add a decorative touch to your books. If you have doors on your bookcase, house unattractive items there, such as board games, catalogs, boxes of photos, greeting cards, stationery, cassette tapes, compact discs, or videos. Explore the possibilities. If you keep a few toys for visiting children, this is a handy place to keep them too.

Coffee Tables—Consider one with storage possibilities. Many have shelves or drawers. A large trunk can also serve as a coffee table and furnish space for blankets, catalogs, games, videos, or gift-wrapping supplies.

End Tables—Shelves or drawers are often found in end tables as well. Make good use of them to keep the TV remote, pens, paper, tissues, hand lotion, or whatever you find yourself needing when sitting in the living room.

Establishing Limits

Recreational Items—When the video cabinet is full, it's time to weed out some of the videos and slow down or stop buying new ones. The same goes for games, toys, and books. Determine how much space you have for these items. If you truly don't have enough storage space, plan to increase storage with the purchase of shelving, cabinets, or the like. Once those spaces are filled, weed out the unused items before adding more.

Decorative Items—Keep decorations simple for best effect. "Simple" is easier to dust, and each item stands out more if there aren't so many things to look at that. Large items pack more punch than myriad tiny things and once again, are easier to clean. Photographs are one thing people tend to let accumulate because they can't bear to take them down (especially grandmas). Try to limit how many photos you display, and when a new one is given to you, put it in a frame you already have hanging. Take out the old photo and put it in a photo album that you can browse through at your leisure. The photo will mean even more to you when you haven't seen it in a while.

Laundry Room

Organized Storage

Shelving/Cabinets—At the very minimum, install a shelf above the washer and dryer to store detergent and laundry supplies. If your laundry area is a separate room or part of a basement or garage, it's a great place to store miscellaneous items. Line the walls with inexpensive shelving or old cabinets from someone's remodeling project to store an iron, sewing equipment, craft supplies, houseplant supplies, home maintenance items, or pet supplies. If shelving is open, use well-marked plastic or cardboard boxes to organize items and keep them clean. A large open shelf or the top of the cabinets can store coolers, water jugs, etc. Vases or large seldom-used kitchen items, such as roasters or stock pots, can be stored here as well as reusable items such as coffee cans and glass jars. A box for clothes that are too small can stay here until it's full and ready to be passed on.

Laundry Baskets—Baskets help organize the laundry area. Sort dirty clothes into baskets, then use the empty baskets to transport clean, folded clothes to bedrooms.

Cleaning Instructions—No matter how we try to simplify, there will be certain items that have specific cleaning instructions. These items might include blankets, quilts, rugs, or pillows. Many times, you don't want to leave that big tag attached to such visible items. Instead, tear off the tag and put it in a small notebook. Clearly mark what item the tag belongs to and keep the notebook in your laundry area. When you need to wash a special item, you can look up the instructions.

Establishing Limits

Remember not to bother organizing things you'll never use. Seriously examine your collections of craft supplies, fabric, sewing notions, and hobby materials. Keep only three or four coffee cans and glass jars; they are readily available for replacement if you find yourself needing more for a particular project (such as organizing nails and screws). Don't bog yourself down with unlimited stuff. Keep a few needed items and weed out the rest. If you haven't used an item in more than a year, pass it on to someone who will.

Office

Organized Storage

Desk—Make maximum use of your desk. Don't take up space with things you seldom use. Your desktop should have more empty work space than clutter. Line the far edge with frequently needed items such as a telephone, letter trays, a lamp, stapler, tape dispenser, pencil cup, notepad, and calculator. Keep the working portion of your desk free of clutter so you can work. Use the letter trays to store frequently used papers and telephone books. Put other papers away in a file or on a bulletin board. Your drawers should hold items you need often such as pens, markers, scissors, paper clips, a ruler, staple remover, Wite-Out, glue, an address book, checkbook, envelopes, stamps, and stationery.

Bulletin Board—Install one above your desk for miscellaneous papers such as party invitations, concert tickets, directions to the family reunion, or anything temporarily important. If it's not temporary, file it in an appropriate place. Other candidates include school or church calendars, community event flyers, voting information, letters to answer, etc. Don't overload it to the point that it is no longer functional, however. As items become outdated, throw them away.

Filing Cabinets—Every home needs at least two file drawers. If your desk contains a large file drawer, don't fill it with useless junk; purchase some file folders and set up the drawer for its intended purpose. Create folders for bills, receipts, medical records, and so on. If you don't have file drawers, purchase a filing cabinet with at least two drawers. Inexpensive ones can be found at discount stores, or scout around for a used one if cost is a concern. Another important investment is a fireproof box to store valuable papers. These come in various sizes from a three-inch deep box to a large safe. You'll find them at office supply stores.

Establishing Limits

Files—Separate files into four types, based on importance. Fireproof files are the most valuable, and need to be kept indefinitely; permanent files need to be kept as long as they are pertinent; annual files need to be kept for the current year; and activity files need to be kept as long as you determine.

Fireproof files should include your will, insurance policies, cash, savings passbooks, safe-deposit box keys, deeds, titles, stocks, bonds, passports, and important contracts. Some of these may need to be kept in both a fireproof box and a safe-deposit box. You should have several valid, notarized copies of your will. Tell your attorney and your executor where your copies are located, not just "in this gray box," but where the box is kept in your home, and at which bank your safe-deposit box is located.

Permanent files should include automobile records, home maintenance records, loan records, tax records, résumés, and medical records. These records are for major assets or long-term liabilities. When you no longer own an asset, the file can be destroyed. Some information, such as maintenance records, should be given to the new owner should you sell your house or car. Be sure to go through the file and eliminate any personal information before passing it on. Long-term liability records need to be kept one year after they are paid off. If the liability incurred tax-deductible interest, keep an interest statement with your tax records.

Taxes indeed qualify as long-term liabilities! The government requires tax records to be kept for three years. Pocket folders are handy files for tax records. Keep receipts on one side and your copies of the completed forms on the other. The folders will fit in a standard hanging file, although they stick up a bit. Store the folder open end up, and write the year in bold black marker on the portion that sticks up. Keep these in back of the file drawer so they don't block your view of the other file tabs, and because they are seldom needed.

Annual files include bank statements, credit card statements, insurance bills, utility bills, and any type of bills or receipts that do not need to be kept permanently. At the end of the year, these files can be emptied to use for the new year. Be careful, though. If any records are tax deductible, such as utility bills for a home office, the receipts must be kept for the three-year minimum as tax records.

Activity files include anything you are currently involved or interested in. If you are house hunting, set up a file for housing information. Committees you serve on or activities you are involved in may require that you keep paperwork or information handy. Keep a school file to store notes from the teacher, a telephone directory, the school handbook, or the like. Similarly, a church file could store the church constitution, membership directory, annual report, or other important information. If you like to keep articles or information on hobbies such as crafts, sewing, gardening, decorating, or even Christmas ideas, make a file for it, and when you need an idea you can simply look it up. This requires far less space than saving piles of magazines; tear out only particular articles that interest you and file them away.

Color Code—The easiest way to keep track of what files are is to color-code them. You can buy colored file folders or colored file labels. You can also use highlighters to color-code the file tabs yourself, or you can use colored markers to label the files—one color for each type of file.

Keep like files together and alphabetize within each category. The color coding will make misfiling very obvious. Either have a separate drawer for each type of files, or one type at the front and another type at the back of a drawer.

Junk Mail—Do you realize a good percentage of clutter has literally zero value? Piles of junk mail, old newspapers, magazines, and catalogs clutter up homes faster than anything else. Cut down on junk mail by minimizing how many mailing lists you are on. Occasionally a company will ask you if you want to be on their mailing list; think it over before saying yes. When you get the mail, sit near a trash can and throw away the junk mail immediately.

Regular Mail—Separate mail into three piles: bills to pay, things to read now, and things to read later. Put the bills in your file for paperwork day, read what you plan to read now, and set aside things to read later in a convenient place where you can look at them while relaxing in the evening. Cancel any newspaper or magazine subscriptions you don't have time to read. It's a waste of money to have these lying around unread until you get disgusted and throw them out. Don't be suckered into replacing them, either!

Basement

Organized Storage

Arrange It as a Room—Basements are a mixed blessing. If you have an unfinished basement, the storage possibilities are endless (although sometimes that's a problem!). The best remedy for "pack-rat-itis" is to consider your basement a room. It is one, after all. You wouldn't set boxes in the middle of the floor in any other room, would you? If you are storing old furniture, arrange it as any other room would be arranged. This helps the area look neat and keeps you mindful that it is a room.

Use It as a Room—If you long for an office, a sewing room, a craft room, workshop, greenhouse, recreation room, or playroom, turn the basement into one. Don't let a lack of funds to finish the room properly keep you from using it. With little or no cash, and a lot of ingenuity, this can become a useful space. Use what you have. Any table can be used for a desk, sewing or craft table, work bench or potting area. Install fluorescent lights or grow lights from the rafters, or use an old lamp. Any bookcase or metal shelving unit will store supplies.

A recreation room or playroom doesn't require a lot of furniture. Bring some toys downstairs, especially big items such as toy kitchens and workbenches, race tracks, and train sets. Some shelves are helpful to keep things neat. Any old furniture you have or can scrounge can be used for sitting, or you can use bean bag chairs, large pillows, or even an old mattress (kids would love that!). We turned our basement into a playroom for no money at all. We had an old love seat, a beat-up coffee table, an old crib, a bookcase, and a play rug. We arranged these items as a room. The crib holds stuffed animals, the love seat and coffee table are set up for a tea party, the bookcase holds miscellaneous toys and books, and the rug provides a place to play with cars.

Space heaters can be added for heat. Throw rugs or an area rug will warm the floor. A coat of paint will brighten the room dramatically. Old pictures or posters will dress up the walls and a few plants will add life. Now isn't this better than all those cardboard boxes full of junk?

Shelving—Admittedly, there will probably be some boxes of stuff you really can't part with; Christmas decorations and seasonal items top the list. Those boxes of tax records don't help, either. Limit the storage areas of your basement to shelving units. Industrial metal shelving can be purchased inexpensively at home improvement centers and can be painted bright colors to liven up this dreary space. You can even section off one area as a storage area and place shelving units in rows like a mini warehouse. This will free up space in the rest of the room to use for other purposes. If you eventually decide to finish the basement, this area could be made into a permanent storage room. If you don't care for this idea, keep the shelving units along the walls. Items kept in open shelving should be in well-marked boxes to keep them organized and clean. If you come across old cabinets from someone's remodeling project, grab them for use in your basement or garage.

Garage

Organized Storage

Shelving—Industrial metal shelving units are a must for any garage. Many items can be neatly stored this way, so keep like things together. One shelving unit could be set aside for auto supplies; another for home repair items. Keep gardening supplies and insecticides together. Keep sports equipment, toys, and pet supplies together in a separate area. Always reserve top shelves for chemicals or items dangerous to children or pets.

Bins—Small items such as nails and screws should be kept in bins (coffee cans work well) to keep them sorted. Paint the cans bright colors so they are quickly recognized, and label them clearly as well. Cover sharp edges with duct tape for safety.

Pegboard—Large tools such as shovels, rakes, hoes, hedge clippers, and saws can be stored on pegboard. Anything sharp should be kept out of reach of children.

Hooks—Screw large hooks into the wall or ceiling for storage of bicycles, power tools, weed trimmers, ladders, sawhorses, or other large items to get them off the floor.

Work Bench—Some type of bench or table is useful as a work area. Keep needed tools and supplies nearby.

Tool Box—Organization of tools is critical when trying to get a job done. A basic tool box should include a hammer, straight and Phillips screwdrivers, tape measure, crescent wrench, pliers, electrical tape, and, of course, duct tape. A ratchet and sockets would be necessary if you work on your own car. (Speaking of your car, now that the garage is organized, maybe you can actually park it there!)

Getting Rid of the Excess

Once you have gone through the entire house, what do you do with all that extra unwanted (and unnecessary) stuff? Do you keep it, sell it, give it away, or toss it? If you use an item often, keep it. If it has such sentimental value you'd be heartbroken without it, keep it. (Let's not go overboard with the sentimentality, though. Isn't that how all this stuff got here in the first place?) If you haven't used an item for more than a year, it's of no use to you; get rid of it. If it has enough value that you cannot afford to give it away without regret, sell it. If it has value, but you can give it away without regret, give it away. If it has no value, throw it away!

Your Options

Garage sale—If you decide to go through the effort of having a garage sale, be prepared. Allow sufficient time for sorting, pricing, and set up. Advertise in the local paper, and put up signs in advance. Attach balloons to your mailbox and put large signs in the front yard. Make sure you have lots of change—more than you think you'll need. Be sure to count your change beforehand so you know what you started with. Have a calculator, paper, and pencil handy. Fill a cooler with sandwiches and drinks so you won't be hungry. Enlist at least one helper for hectic times and bathroom breaks. If you have young children, enlist another helper for child care, or let them visit grandma or a friend.

After the sale, give the leftovers to friends. You could even give away items to customers during the last hour of the sale (or drastically reduce prices). Whatever you do, don't you dare take that stuff back into the house! You've already cleaned it out once, don't do it again. Give the rest to charity after your friends have looked through it.

Classifieds—If you have valuable items (such as furniture, appliances, sports equipment, tools, electronics, antiques, jewelry, or expensive clothing), run a classified ad for those specific items instead of organizing a huge sale.

Charity—Find a local charity and frequent it. Some charities will even pick up items at your home, which saves you considerable trouble. I keep a large cardboard box in the basement for things we no longer use—the "Give Away Box." When we come across clothing that's too small, knick-knacks we no longer want, or kitchen gadgets we no longer use, we put them in the box. When the box is full, it goes to our local charity. This method keeps unwanted items from piling up and eliminates the need for a garage sale.

Friends and Family—If you know someone who would appreciate your discarded items, especially children's clothing or toys, then by all means, pass them along. Be absolutely certain, however, that they genuinely appreciate the items. Give them the option of saying no. You can also offer to let them pick and choose items they could use, and then give the rest to charity.

Other Recipients—A local crisis pregnancy center would undoubtedly appreciate baby items. A doctor's office, auto dealership, lawyer, or accountant's office might appreciate magazines for the waiting room, especially if you've noticed their selections are lacking. A school may appreciate kitchen items for the home economics class, toys for kindergarten or preschool, and craft supplies for art projects. A church can often use baby items, toys, and children's books for the nursery, kitchen items for the kitchen, tools for church maintenance, and Christian books, magazines, or videos for the library. Always call these places beforehand to avoid putting them on the spot if they really aren't interested, and don't be offended if they aren't.

Recycling—Actually, what I'm referring to here is reusing. Many items can be used over and over. Let me warn you, however. If you keep too many of these things on hand, you will defeat your purpose of simplifying and organizing. Allow a set amount of space for such extra items and when it is full, that's it. Many of these items, however, can be used as storage containers, so they are not taking up additional space.

Baskets can be used to serve rolls, muffins, or cookies. They can hold plasticware for a picnic. They can be filled with styrofoam and used for potting silk plants or flowers. They can also be lined with plastic and used to hold a live potted plant. They can hold pencils, crayons, art supplies, makeup, bath products, extra rolls of toilet paper, magazines, newspapers, stationery, stickers, toys, candy, apples, or dog bones. They can be used as gift baskets too.

Margarine tubs are wonderful items to have around. They can be used to store leftovers, or to share your leftovers with guests. (No need for them to return the container!) They are also great for holding buttons, safety pins, sewing notions, rubber bands, paper clips, push pins, etc. Put some in your tool box to organize it. Lidless tubs can be put in your desk drawer or junk drawer to keep things orderly.

Glass jars can be used to hold some of the same items. Although they are breakable, you can see through them and they can hold paint, thinner, stain, and the like that cannot be stored in plastic. Keep several extra glass jars in the garage for mixing paint. Glass jars also make wonderful old-fashioned vases. Tie a ribbon around the rim to cover it. Fill with flowers and enjoy!

Coffee cans are wonderful for the garage. Be sure to file any sharp edges or cover the edges with duct tape. The cans are indestructible and great for holding nails, screws, and miscellaneous hardware. You can also use them as large scoops for potting soil, fertilizer, dog food, or rock salt for melting ice. A large coffee can filled with sand makes a good outdoor ashtray to keep the butts out of your yard.

As you review the storage ideas in this chapter, try some of them out. Photocopy the following page and add it to your daily planner. Then start organizing! Review the page at the end of the week and month, then fill out another page.

She watches over the affairs of her household
and does not eat the bread of idleness.
Proverbs 31:27

Organizing Your Home

Organizing to Do Today:

_____

_____

_____

Organizing to Do This Week:

_____

_____

_____

Organizing to Do This Month:

_____

_____

_____

Organizing to Do This Year:

_____

_____

_____

Getting Things Done

Whatever you do, work at it with all your
heart, as working for the Lord, not for men.
Colossians 3:23

Procrastination

The only way to eliminate procrastination is to do
your work first. Think of your day like a meal. First, eat
your salad, then your main course, and save your dessert
for last. Salad is preparation, the main course gets you into
the heart of the matter, and dessert is savoring the fruits of
your labor—resting.

Preparation—Preparation for any job should
include prayer. Pray for God's help in accomplishing what
needs to be done today. When you really have a lot to do,
you don't have time not to pray. You need God's assistance
and His blessing on your day. Never consider prayer time
procrastination; consider it preparation.

The second phase of preparation is physically getting
ready for the job. Getting dressed, eating breakfast, and

straightening up the work area are all parts of preparation. Assembling necessary tools or supplies for the job is also part of the preparation.

Work with Your Style—If you are not a morning person, it's OK! God made each of us differently. Work with your style. If you just can't seem to delve into a major project at the crack of dawn, then do a few smaller jobs first to wind yourself up. Preparations are perfect for this. Go over your to-do list and get yourself motivated. Once again, prayer definitely helps. Imagine how nice it will be at the end of the day to enjoy the satisfaction of a job well done. Look forward to that sense of accomplishment as a means of motivating yourself to get on with the job at hand.

If you are a morning person, by all means jump right into your work. Get your major jobs out of the way and do smaller jobs later when you're running out of steam. You may even want to go over your to-do list for the next day and begin the necessary preparations. Work with your style. But whatever you do, keep focused on your goals for the day and do not allow yourself to get off track with other tasks or relaxing activities such as television or reading.

Work Diligently—Once you are prepared, you can begin your work. Work diligently, as working for the Lord. Stay focused on getting this job done today. If you have planned properly and not expected too much of yourself for one day, then you can pace yourself and work toward the goals you are hoping to achieve. Set minor goals throughout the day; for example, I want to have the bathroom clean by lunch time and the bedrooms and living room done this afternoon. While preparing dinner, I'll work on cleaning up the kitchen. Effective planning helps thwart procrastination.

Fruits of Your Labor—Now that your work is done, you can enjoy your just desserts—relaxing after dinner and knowing that you have accomplished your goals today. What a wonderful feeling.

Intimidation

Experience Is the Best Teacher—Often we are too intimidated to start a task because we just don't know how to do it. Many times, however, the only way to learn how is to jump in and get our feet wet. Once we begin, many of the steps will logically follow. We may make mistakes but we will learn from them. You'll be surprised how many things you can learn to do just by getting in there and doing them. If you get stuck, consult someone with experience or borrow a library book that offers instructions. Libraries are a treasure trove of information. And they're free! Landscaping, gardening, building a deck, auto repairs, home repairs, upholstery, sewing, crafts, cake decorating, painting techniques, calligraphy, and how to fly an airplane are just a few of the things you can learn from books.

Practice Makes Perfect—Sometimes we know how to do a job but we feel inadequate. (It takes me too long, I can't do it as well as someone else, and so on.) Even the experts started right where you are; there was a first time for everyone. To become good at something, we have to work at it. We will never achieve greatness if we don't begin. Your first project may not be wonderful but it will be a learning experience for you. The next one will be better, and the next one will be better yet.

Fear of Failure—Maybe you're intimidated because you're afraid you'll ultimately fail. If you don't try, you'll be certain to fail. You will fail because you were afraid to try. If a child refuses to take a test because of fear, guess what? The teacher gives an F. This isn't school, this is life; but even so, we have a Teacher who expects us to try. Read

Matthew 25:14–30; Jesus' parable illustrates how God wants us to use the gifts and talents He's given us.

Don't be intimidated! Just do it, one step at a time. God will help you. "For God did not give us a spirit of timidity, but a spirit of power, of love and of self-discipline" (2 Timothy 1:7).

Maximum Efficiency

Do Two Things at Once—You can save time by doing more than one thing at the same time. Work smarter, not harder. Be efficient and have fun. Do things together with others. Errands and shopping can be done in the same trip; get together with a friend and get haircuts together; go to a friend's house and help her paint the kitchen, then invite her over to help you paint yours. No time to see your friends at Christmas? Have a cookie-baking party! Everyone gets their cookies baked and you get to visit as well. You could do the same thing for tree trimming, ornament making, gift wrapping, or Christmas card writing. Share supplies, and everyone will get to try something new. This practice all but eliminates boredom and saves hours of time.

Buy a Cordless Phone—Many, many things can be done while on the phone, including washing the dishes, cooking dinner, putting groceries away, baking cookies, folding laundry, mopping the floor, dusting the furniture, or straightening up the house.

Delegate—If your family isn't helping around the house, it's about time they started. Rule number one is picking up after yourself, including toys, clothes, dirty dishes, and whatever else is left around. When you get up from the dinner table, you take your plate with you. Scrape food scraps into the trash and put the dishes in the sink. Children can do this as soon as they can reach the sink. If dirty dishes are left in the living room, the children are summoned from the far reaches of the house to pick them up; it is their job. Putting their clean clothes away is also their job. You can wash the clothes; the kids can put them away. Keeping their own rooms clean and cleaning up their own messes are other chores that children (and husbands) can help with. There's no rule against mom helping out, but ultimately each child needs to learn responsibility. The milk will be spilled far less often if the spiller has to clean it up.

Husbands tend to be more willing to help if:

1. We don't criticize the way they do the job.

2. We allow them flexibility to make their own decisions.

3. We show genuine appreciation for a job that's done (even if it's not the way we would have done it).

4. We ask! Ask nicely for help, and you might be surprised at the response. Don't nag.

If asking nicely is not working, have a talk with your husband. Choose a time when you're not upset. Don't try to discuss it when you're frantic. In that situation, you're bound to say something you'll later regret. It will take a lot longer to help him see your point of view if he has been insulted. When timing is appropriate, explain to your husband that you would really appreciate a little help. Remember to state how you feel about the issue, rather than accusing or insulting him. "I feel like I have to do everything by myself" is a lot easier to take than "you never do anything." Think over your main points beforehand so that you have a clear argument for why he really needs to help out. Examples could be "I work all day too, and it's not fair that I'm the only one doing all of the housework," or "the children are a handful and I can't make dinner with them hanging on me the entire time." Evaluate your situation and state clear reasons why you need help.

Prepare for his arguments. Honestly ask yourself a few questions. Do you think maybe he doesn't help because you yell at him every time he tries? If so, tell him you are aware of how you've acted, you are sorry, and that you are trying to do better. And mean it. Do you feel maybe he doesn't help because you haven't been so cooperative with him? Offering to help him with jobs that he has to do, or offering to do something he likes to do with him is a wonderful incentive. Sure, it's bargaining. But it's a win-win situation.

Pray for your husband, pray for patience, and pray that you will be kind and say the right things. Be sure to notice any improvements made, and thank him. The best thanks of all is a smile, a hug, and a loving disposition.

Getting children to help is sometimes easier than husbands. Motivation is simple—avoid a spanking or other punishment. Children should be responsible for helping around the house; they will never learn responsibility for anything if we don't teach it to them.

Turn Off the Tube—Watching television can be a wonderfully relaxing rest period, or it can be a black hole of time. Like most things in life, it's fine in moderation. A few hours in the evening is restful before bed, it's great to watch a movie or catch the news. But don't leave it on all day. Television is addictive; start watching it and you'll have a hard time getting anything done. If you need something as "background noise," try the radio. (Just be careful what station you pick; an interesting program on talk radio can be just as distracting as TV!)

Screen Calls—So you don't have a secretary to screen your calls? Your children are too young, you say? But do you own an answering machine? These wonderful devices can take messages for you while you are busy getting something done. If it's important, you can either pick up immediately or call back. If it's a salesperson, a wrong number, or just not important, they'll hang up. Tell your immediate family that this is your practice, and if they have an urgent call to leave a message.

Projects

Plan Ahead—Use your daily planner to schedule time for a major project. Don't even try to get a large project like painting or wallpapering done in one day. Schedule projects for times when your family is at work and school. Why spend the weekend painting if you don't have to? Many people are afraid to tackle large projects on their own. Get some pointers from someone who's done the job, or research it. There are magazine articles on everything from sponge painting to planting roses. Visit the library and look into home improvements, gardening, landscaping, or whatever. Decorating magazines are wonderful sources of information; you can get them at the library too. After your research, go back to your daily planner and write down the supplies you'll need on your shopping list. Then plan easy meals for those project days, whether they be takeout, a Crock-Pot meal, leftovers, or sandwiches.

Break It Down into Manageable Steps—Make a list of the steps needed to complete the job and check them off as you finish them. Steps will include research, buying supplies, preparation, the steps involved in the job itself, and cleaning up. Plan a tentative schedule, estimating how long each step will take. If this is your first attempt at the project, overestimate. Give yourself plenty of time so you are not rushed and end up making mistakes. Major projects such as painting, wallpapering, or planting a garden will probably take more than one day from preparation to the finished job. And remember, the job's not complete until everything is cleaned up, put away, and rearranged the way it should be.

Use the Right Tools—The right tool for the job makes it easier and faster to complete. In some cases, the job is impossible to complete without that tool; in others, the job will never be quite right without the proper tool. This doesn't just apply to working on cars. Home repairs, painting, even cooking and baking are much simpler with the tools of the trade. And the better quality the tools are, the easier it will be to get good results. If you want a professional job, use professional tools.

Methods

God's Way—Remember what we talked about in chapter 2? Plans contrary to God's plan don't work. Equally important are the methods we use to carry out God's plan. While it is important to get things done, be certain you are using God's methods to carry out His will. It is entirely possible to be doing God's will but not in God's way.

God's Method—Let's look to King David for an example. He planned to bring the ark of the covenant back to Jerusalem once he became king; this was God's will. But God had set rules for how to move the ark many years earlier. Deuteronomy 10:8 reports: "At that time the LORD set apart the tribe of Levi to carry the ark of the covenant of the LORD." More detailed instructions on *how* to carry it are recorded in Exodus.

David's Method—King David did not move the ark God's way. He used modern methods, the same methods the Philistines had used. We find the story in 1 Samuel 6:7–8: "Now then, get a new cart ready, with two cows that have calved and have never been yoked. Hitch the cows to the cart … Take the ark of the LORD and put it on the cart …" David used the same method when he brought the ark back after defeating the Philistines. See 2 Samuel 6:3: "They set the ark of God on a new cart …" This caused some problems, as we find in 2 Samuel 6:6–7: "Uzzah reached out and took hold of the ark of God, because the oxen stumbled. The LORD's anger burned against Uzzah because of his irreverent act; therefore God struck him down and he died there beside the ark of God."

David Learns a Lesson—David admits his mistake when he speaks to the Levites in 1 Chronicles 15:12–13: "You and your fellow Levites are to consecrate yourselves and bring up the ark of the LORD, the God of Israel, to the place I have prepared for it. It was because you, the Levites, did not bring it up the first time that the LORD our God broke out in anger against us. We did not inquire of Him about how to do it in the prescribed way."

Disaster Prevention—God's methods are the only proper way to carry out His will. If we don't consult Him, disastrous results are likely.

Think about what you need to get done. Pray about how to do it. As you are planning your to-do list, photocopy the following page and add it to your daily planner. You may wish to make several photocopies of this page.

Always give yourselves fully to the work
of the Lord, because you know that your
labor in the Lord is not in vain.
1 Corinthians 15:58

Getting Things Done

Jobs I Need to Do:

_____

_____

_____

_____

_____

_____

_____

Steps I Need to Take:

_____

_____

_____

_____

_____

_____

Simple Pleasures

Go, eat your food with gladness,
and drink your wine with a joyful heart,
for it is now that God favors what you do.
Ecclesiastes 9:7

Freedom

Free Time—Congratulations! Now that you are simplifying your schedule and getting your home in order, you will be able to free up some time to truly enjoy those blessings God has given you. It's a shame that so many people view planning and order as boundaries on their personal freedom. The exact opposite is true! Those boundaries are what keep demanding schedules and work from overtaking our lives, resulting in no freedom at all! Free time is available to anyone; it is achieved by properly managing time and setting boundaries on those things that consume time.

Creating order is a lifelong process. You have begun the process by reading this book, filling in the pages at the end of each chapter, and using a daily planner. As you embark upon a new lifestyle of simplification and organization, don't forget the purpose of it all—to enjoy life more! Simple pleasures happen every day. With some of your new free time, look around for those pleasures you were always too busy to enjoy before you got organized!

God's Blessings for Us

God Himself—The most precious blessing of God is God Himself. He wants nothing but to love you, protect you, and bring you to Himself. "The LORD your God is with you, He is mighty to save. He will take great delight in you, He will quiet you with His love, He will rejoice over you with singing" (Zephaniah 3:17).

Appreciate the blessings of knowing God and His love. Thank Him for your salvation. Seek His guidance, His comfort, and His peace. Commune with Him daily through Bible study and prayer. " 'You will seek Me and find Me when you seek Me with all your heart. I will be found by you,' declares the LORD" (Jeremiah 29:13–14).

Simple Pleasures to Enjoy with God

- **Pray. Talk to God and tell Him how you feel today.**
- **Read Bible passages that comfort you.**
- **Meditate on God's Word.**
- **Memorize Scripture.**
- **Worship at your favorite church.**
- **Praise God by singing songs or hymns.**
- **Praise God by reading the Psalms aloud.**
- **Thank God for all His blessings to you.**
- **Share your blessings with God by giving back a portion for His work.**

Loved Ones—Learn to truly appreciate your loved ones; all too often we take them for granted. Make a conscious effort to cherish your husband, children, parents, sisters, brothers, extended family, and friends. Look for their best qualities and dwell on those, overlooking any faults that distort your view of who they really are. Remind yourself often how fortunate you are to have these people in your life. Spend as much time as possible with them and treat them with respect and kindness, all the more so your husband and children—those closest to you.

When you fail and lose your temper, apologize. Tell them often how much you love them. Hold them close in your heart and in your arms. Catch your children being good—and praise them. Be aware of all that your husband does for you. Gifts, dinners out, and special occasions are wonderful, but we need to gain an appreciation for the ordinary things, small gifts we receive every day.

Simple Pleasures to Enjoy with Your Loved Ones

- **Sleep in.**
- **Give each other back rubs.**
- **Cuddle.**
- **Watch cartoons with the children.**
- **Nestle your children on your lap.**
- **Listen to your husband laugh.**
- **Reminisce with an old friend or a family member.**
- **Fill photo albums; look through the old ones.**
- **Tell your children stories about your youth.**
- **Listen to your children play.**
- **Visit the playground and see who can swing the highest.**
- **Go to the zoo.**
- **Visit an amusement park.**

- Go to the park and play baseball.
- Fly a kite.
- Catch bugs and butterflies.
- Kick a soccer ball around the yard.
- Play tennis or badminton.
- Take a fishing trip.
- Go swimming.
- Walk on the beach and find shells.
- Visit interesting places in your neighborhood.
- Go miniature golfing.
- Dance with your husband.
- Go bowling.
- Go roller skating.
- Take a leisurely walk—let the children pick up sticks, etc., that they find along the way.
- Hike through the woods or up a mountain.
- Pick wildflowers.
- Go camping.
- Take a drive in the country; smell the cows!
- Drive past a vineyard and smell the grapes (much more pleasant than cows).
- Rake leaves and jump in them.
- Make leaf people by stuffing old clothes with leaves and using pumpkins for heads.
- Carve jack-o-lanterns.
- Ride sleds or toboggans down a snow-covered hill.
- Go ice-skating.
- Make a snowman or snow angels.
- Drive around town to look at Christmas lights.
- Go window shopping.

- Exercise together.
- Work on crafts together.
- Play board games. Try Monopoly, Checkers, Uno, Scrabble, or Yahtzee.
- Have a water balloon fight.
- Jump in mud puddles.
- Pour bubble solution into a large pan and use slotted spoons to blow giant bubbles.
- Take a vacation!

Home—Our homes are shared with our families. When they are peaceful and comfortable havens filled with love, they become a place the whole family loves to come home to.

Simple Pleasures to Enjoy Your Home

- Decorate with your favorite things.
- Create cozy seating with colorful cushions.
- Make a comfy bed with a thick comforter and plump pillows.
- Honor your family with a photo gallery on a wall or tabletop.
- Design a pretty floral centerpiece for your table.
- Arrange an assortment of fruits in a large bowl.
- Set up a collection of candlesticks in the fireplace for summer.
- Burn candles for a romantic glow.
- Light a fire for cozy warmth and atmosphere.
- Set potpourri in a pretty dish for beauty and fragrance.
- Decorate bedrooms to suit the inhabitants.
- Add plants or flowers for a breath of fresh air.
- Hang colorful pictures to add cheer.

- Cover windows in lightweight fabrics for maximum sunlight.
- Display collectibles on shelves or tables.
- Scatter books about to encourage reading.
- Throw an afghan over the sofa to snuggle in.
- Bake something yummy for a wonderful aroma.

Yourself—Our bodies are also blessings from God. Appreciate your health, strength, mobility, flexibility, adaptability, intellect, sexuality, sight, hearing, sense of smell, taste, and touch. "For You created my inmost being; You knit me together in my mother's womb. I praise You because I am fearfully and wonderfully made; Your works are wonderful, I know that full well" (Psalm 139:13–14).

Focus on the intangible aspects of yourself as well as the physical: love, peace, joy, wisdom, and faith. Recognize your individual strengths and strive to overcome your weaknesses. Appreciate your unique gifts and use them.

Simple Pleasures to Enjoy by Yourself

- Soak in a bubble bath.
- Take a cool shower.
- Give yourself a facial.
- Get a manicure or pedicure.
- Get your hair done in a salon.
- Dress up in fun or pretty clothes.
- Dress down in comfy clothes.
- Do stretching exercises.
- Enjoy crisp, clean sheets.
- Take a nap.
- Cuddle up in a warm blanket.
- Listen to your favorite music.
- Enjoy poetry.

- Write in a journal.
- Lose yourself in a good book.
- Learn a new skill.
- Study an interesting subject.
- Take a challenging class.
- Visit an art gallery.
- Browse through your favorite shop.
- Take a day off to relax: sleep in, wear sweats, lounge around, read, watch TV, work on a hobby, listen to music, and eat your favorite foods.

Creation—Appreciate the wonder of creation. Observe the world around you; use all five senses to soak in its beauty. Every season of the year has individual aspects God created for our enjoyment. Have you noticed lately? How long has it been since you jumped in a pile of fallen leaves and reveled in their woodsy smell and their joyful crunchiness? Try it again! Examine a handful of snowflakes to see the differences in each one. Break off a big, long icicle and taste it. Grab your umbrella and sing in the rain. Better yet, forget the umbrella and lift your face to feel the cool rain refresh you! Do these ideas sound childish to you? There's a little child in each of us, wanting to shout just for the sheer joy of living. Reconnect with that inner child and learn to rejoice in life again.

Simple Pleasures to Enjoy with God's Creation

- Watch a sunset.
- Sit under the stars.
- Listen to night sounds.
- Catch fireflies.
- Smell fresh country air.
- Listen to a babbling brook.

- Enjoy the cool shade of a big tree.
- Go horseback riding.
- View a beautiful garden.
- Listen to a bumble bee.
- Smell freshly mown grass.
- Listen to the wind.
- Watch a caterpillar climb a tree.
- Feed wild birds.
- Walk barefoot on the beach.
- Taste the salt air of the ocean.
- Listen to the crashing waves.
- Set up a tropical fish aquarium.
- Visit an arboretum.
- Crunch through the woods on a bright fall day.
- Listen to a thunderstorm.
- Slide on the walk after an ice storm.
- Taste snowflakes as they float down.

Work—Yes, work is a blessing from God. Without work, there would be no purpose, no challenge, nothing to do. Life would be boring and meaningless. You need not be a doctor, lawyer, business person, or clergy; all work is important, including raising children, keeping house, changing diapers, or taking out the trash. All work is necessary for the common good. Take pride and pleasure in your work, whatever it is.

Simple Pleasures to Enjoy Your Work

- Plan your work and work your plan.
- Appreciate your accomplishments each step of the way.
- Take the time to do the job right.

- Sing or listen to music.
- Maintain good rapport with coworkers.
- Take pleasure in the task.
- Acknowledge the importance of your work.
- Enjoy the satisfaction of a job well done.
- Make every effort to do what you love.

Holidays

How do you simplify (and thus *enjoy*) the holidays without feeling like Scrooge? First of all, remember what Scrooge learned—people are more important than money and work. Spend more time with people you love, less time working and spending money, and the holidays will be great! (And no one will call you Scrooge!)

Plan Ahead—The key to a full and enjoyable holiday season is planning well in advance of the month of December. Shopping can be done throughout the year, when you see an item that someone would like. This is easier on the budget too. Make a list of the people you buy for and keep it in your planner. When you buy a gift, cross that name off the list and don't be tempted to buy additional gifts.

Try to have the shopping done by the beginning of December. Work on Christmas cards and letters during November so you can mail them early in December. The first week of December, decorate. The second week of December, wrap gifts. The third week of December, bake. Then it's Christmas! This routine helps spread out the work but it also helps spread out the season so we can fully enjoy it. Of course, nothing is carved in stone, and things still get hectic. But having some goals for each week gives you focus and helps you organize your time better. Any improvement is a big help.

Decorating—Simple decorations are best. One large poinsettia plant packs more punch than several small displays of knick-knacks. The Christmas tree alone decorates the living room or family room quite well. Put it in the front window and passersby can appreciate it as well. A nice nativity set can be used on a mantle, on top of an entertainment center, on a side table, or under the tree. Buy red, gold, or green candles and a pretty centerpiece for the table (the poinsettia will do) and your dining room is done. A wreath on the door and a garland on the banister finishes the entry.

For outdoor decorations, a large wreath on the front door, some red ribbons on the lampposts, and a few colored floodlights (or your regular outside lights with colored bulbs) are simple, tasteful, and festive. However, if you truly enjoy stringing lights on the bushes and the rooftops, go for it! We'll all enjoy it as we drive by.

Baking—Don't overdo the goodies. It is time-consuming, expensive, and dangerous for your waistline. Put off baking until the week before Christmas. Have the decorating, shopping, and most of the wrapping done by then. Limit yourself to five recipes. Spend a day or two of that week baking, and if there are recipes you don't get done, bake them after the holidays when the other goodies are gone.

Christmas Dinner—To save time in the kitchen and money in the grocery store, have a potluck dinner. Plan a menu and have everyone bring something. Don't overdo it; an appetizer, one meat dish, one potato or pasta dish, two vegetable dishes, bread or rolls, and one dessert is more than plenty! You can decide what dishes you'd like, or just ask some to bring a side dish and others to bring dessert. Let the cook choose her favorite recipe, and your dinner is destined to be delicious.

Forget the turkey; you had one for Thanksgiving. Bake a ham or roast the day before. Slice and arrange it in your nicest shallow baking pan, cover with juice or gravy—

pineapple juice or glaze for ham, canned gravy for a roast. Cover with foil and refrigerate. On Christmas Day, stick the pan in the oven until the meat is warm and tender. It's ready to serve—sliced and in a serving dish. (I make a potato dish that can also be prepared the day before and refrigerated. All I have to do is pop it in the oven. Right before dinner, I microwave the vegetables and dinner is ready.)

Use buffet style for easy service and cleanup. Place silverware and napkins on the tables so no one has to carry them and if you serve drinks before dinner, guests can set them at their places before making a plate. Arrange the kitchen in an orderly fashion, and serving food becomes a breeze. After eating, everyone can carry their own plate to the sink, and if you have several people pitch in, cleaning up goes quickly!

Simple Pleasures to Enjoy All Holidays of the Year

- **Spend the first day of the year with your loved ones.**
- **Bake heart-shaped cookies for Valentine's Day.**
- **Spend February 14 with your soul mate.**
- **Color hard-boiled eggs for Easter.**
- **Read the Resurrection story in Mark 16.**
- **Hide plastic eggs for the children— tuck small tokens in a few.**
- **Attend an Easter Sunrise Service as a family.**
- **Host a BBQ for the Fourth of July.**
- **Attend fireworks after dark.**
- **Have a Labor Day family picnic.**
- **Carve jack-o-lanterns for Halloween.**
- **Pass out candy to trick-or-treaters.**
- **On Thanksgiving, let each family member offer a prayer of thanks for their blessings.**

- Read an Advent calendar each day before Christmas.
- Sing Christmas carols.
- Read the Christmas story in Luke 2.
- Trim the tree together.
- Make a gingerbread house.
- Attend Christmas worship services.
- Entertain some friends for New Year's Eve.
- Serve appetizers and play cards.

Guilt Free

Simple pleasures are yours—guilt free. God has offered you His blessings; He wants you to enjoy them. Appreciate God's goodness, your precious loved ones, the wonder of the human body, the beauty of creation, the rewards of work, and the fruits of your labor. Enjoy good food, a comfortable home, family and friends, and celebrating holidays. All these gifts are yours to enjoy—every day. Each day is a gift from God. Untie the ribbons, unwrap the paper, and embrace the gift!

> Command those who are rich in this present world not to be arrogant nor to put their hope in wealth, which is so uncertain, but to put their hope in God, who richly provides us with everything for our enjoyment. *1 Timothy 6:17*

As you think about all the blessings God has given you, photocopy the following page and add it to your daily planner. List simple pleasures you can enjoy. Thank God for these blessings and opportunities each day.

"Come with Me by yourselves to a quiet place and get some rest." *Mark 6:31*

Simple Pleasures

Simple Pleasures I Can Enjoy Today:

_____

_____

_____

_____

_____

_____

_____

_____

_____

_____

_____

_____

_____

_____

_____

_____

_____

_____

Quick and Easy Meals

Broil or Grill—The broiler or grill is a fast way to cook meats and vegetables. Since the fat drains away from the meat, the resulting meal is lower in fat as well as delicious.

Steak	Chicken
Pork Chops	Fish
Hamburgers	Hot-Dogs
Sausages	Shrimp

Cut-up vegetables can be wrapped in foil to grill. Add seasonings and a little oil or butter. Try potatoes, zucchini, summer squash, mushrooms, carrots, onions, broccoli, or peppers. Remember the wonderful option of shish kabobs! They are fun for the whole family.

Menu:

Any grilled or broiled meat, grilled vegetables, tossed salad, bread or rolls

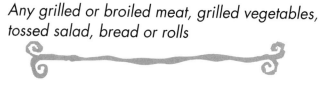

Stove top—Brown ground beef and turn it into: Spaghetti, Beef Stroganoff, Goulash, Sloppy Joes, Tacos, Burritos, Nachos, Chili, or Soup

Menus:

Spaghetti, Beef Stroganoff, or Goulash; green beans, fruit cocktail, garlic bread

Chili or soup, assorted crackers, cheese cubes, carrot & celery sticks, sliced apples

Sloppy Joes, Tacos, Burritos or Nachos; corn with peppers, Mexican style salad, ice-cream sundaes

Stove top—Try these quick entrees for an easy meal:

Chicken Stir Fry	Pepper Steak
Grilled Cheese	BLT
Tuna Melt	Sliced Steak Melt
Smoked Sausage	Reuben

Menus:

Chicken Stir Fry or Pepper Steak, rice and broccoli with cheese, Mandarin oranges

Grilled sandwich, vegetable soup (canned), dill pickle, oatmeal cookies

Sausage or Reuben, sauerkraut, hash browns, baked apples

Cool Summer Solutions—Some days are too hot to even light the grill. Try some of these nice cool meals when it's almost too hot to eat:

Sub Sandwiches	Antipasto
Chef Salad	Tuna Salad
Chicken Salad	Seafood Salad

Menus:

Sub sandwiches, lettuce and tomato, low-fat potato chips, orange

Antipasto, lettuce leaves, bread or rolls, strawberries

Any main dish salad, assorted crackers, fresh pineapple, cottage cheese

Microwave—When we're talking quick and easy, the microwave comes to mind. In addition to the many prepared foods you can buy, you can make many inventive meals using old reliables that are generally healthier and less expensive. Keep an eye out for microwave directions on packaged foods such as rice or pasta dishes. Use the microwave to heat canned or frozen vegetables and to refresh dry bread or rolls. Don't overlook the endless sandwich possibilities. Even a plain ham sandwich takes on a new dimension when turned into "hot ham and cheese." Your supermarket deli offers a host of possibilities besides the obvious and the boring. Other ideas include:

Shaved roast beef with cheese sauce on an onion roll

Roast beef on French bread au jus (beef bouillon)

Shaved turkey on sourdough with salsa and Monterey jack

Open-faced turkey with gravy on toast

Shredded BBQ beef on a hamburger roll with coleslaw

Sliced chicken with onions and peppers on a whole wheat bun

Sliced corned beef and Swiss on pumpernickel

Shaved ham and cheddar on rye

Besides the ordinary sandwich accompaniments of mayonnaise, mustard, and ketchup, remember barbeque sauce, steak sauce, salsa, cheese sauce, horseradish, thousand island, ranch, French, or Italian dressings, gravy, and tartar sauce. For added interest as well as vitamins, add lettuce, tomato, pepper rings, onion, pickles, mushrooms, cucumber, or zucchini. Vegetables can be added cold, warmed in the microwave, or lightly sautéed. Mix and match meats, breads, vegetables, and accompaniments for unique sandwiches that are anything but boring!

Menus:

Any deli sandwich, baked French fries, deli coleslaw

Any deli sandwich, baked soft pretzel, dill pickle

Any deli sandwich, deli potato salad, sliced tomatoes

Make-Ahead Meals

Crock-Pot Meals—Any time of year the Crock-Pot allows you to make dinner early in the day without watching over it or heating up the whole kitchen. It also saves electricity. Any of the ground beef dishes can be prepared early and kept warm in the Crock-Pot. In addition, the following and many more recipes can be started in the morning and will be ready by supper time.

BBQ Short Ribs	Roast Beef and Potatoes
Chicken and Dumplings	Corned Beef and Cabbage
Rigatoni	Swedish Meatballs

Menus:

Any Crock-Pot dish above, green beans, peaches, bread or rolls

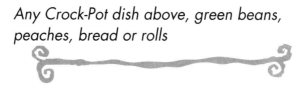

Oven—Many dishes can be prepared the day before or earlier in the day, refrigerated, and placed in the oven an hour or so before mealtime. Any of these can also be prepared in the afternoon and served immediately as well.

Baked Ham	Ham and Scalloped Potatoes
BBQ Ribs	Baked Pork Chops
Sweet and Sour Pork	Roast Pork

Oven Fried Chicken	Chicken and Rice
Roast Chicken	BBQ Chicken Wings
Chicken Chow Mein	Chicken Casserole
Lasagna	Meatloaf
Swiss Steak	Pot Roast
Cabbage Rolls	Beef Brisket
Tuna Casserole	Baked Fish
Deep Dish Pizza	Macaroni and Cheese
Quiche	French Bread Pizza

Menus:

Any meat, mashed potatoes, broccoli and cauliflower, cranberry sauce

Any meat, buttered noodles, peas, Jell-O with fruit

Any casserole, tossed salad, pears, bread or rolls

Any pizza, Caesar salad, fruit cup, cookies

Copy Restaurant Ideas—Many casual restaurants offer unique dishes that are simple to recreate at home. Even if your version isn't quite the same, you may find a delicious alternative that your family will request again and again. Salads and sandwiches in particular are incredibly easy to copy. Just reading the menu can give you wonderful ideas. Now that's a yummy homework assignment!

Simple Decorating Tips

Walls—Pictures are lovely and easier to dust than shelves. Shelves, however, give you dimension and a place to store things. Attractive decorating includes both. Any large wall space could use a picture or shelf to accent it. A grouping of several coordinated pictures looks lovely as an alternative to one large picture. You can also pair a picture and a shelf, or add sconces on either side, or a shelf on one side and a sconce on the other. Mirrors are beautiful and open up a small room. They are also handy near a door to check your hair before going out. Decorative plates are good wall hangings for any room and are easy to clean. Silk plants or flowers add color and texture to shelves. Never place accessories behind a lamp or large plant; rather, use the lamp or plant to accentuate the grouping or to offset it.

To visualize how your wall will look, place the accessories on the floor in front of the wall area and arrange them until you are happy with the look. Measure the size of the grouping and center it on the wall above the furniture. Measure the distance from the ceiling to the grouping on both ends to keep it straight. A small level is an aid, especially for shelves. It helps to have a second person, but you can do this alone. Finally, measure, measure, measure. Use chalk to lightly mark the wall; it wipes right off.

Tabletops—Tabletops can be beautifully decorated using combinations of plants, flowers, figurines, candles, and picture frames. A doily, scarf, or piece of fabric such as a cloth napkin gives a lovely frame to your centerpieces and protects your furniture. The dining room table will need a somewhat large centerpiece; a candle or floral arrangement is fitting. For a country look, use a grapevine wreath set flat on the table, decorated by sticking in silk or dried flowers, artificial fruits or vegetables, and small "picks" available in craft stores. Then place a large candle in the center. You can use a hurricane glass with a thin candle inside or a fat candle set on a saucer. The wreath can be easily changed by removing the picks and replacing them with seasonal varieties. Greens and berries can be used for winter, flowers and seed packets for spring, geraniums and tiny flags for summer, and pumpkins and leaves for fall. Of course, there is an endless supply of decorative items for Christmas. The picks can be stored in plastic bags and take little space. This can be your one seasonal change in decorating.

In the living room, use end tables to hold a lamp or a potted silk plant or flower. You could also display a photo, figurine, or candle, but use only one item in addition to a lamp. You want to accessorize your home, not clutter it. Besides, it is much easier to dust one item than three or four, and it's easier to set down a drink or a book if there's empty space. The top of the entertainment center, if you have one, can be used for larger displays.

Accessories as Storage—We touched on this with the idea of shelves being used as storage in chapter 6. If you have decorative dishes, figurines, or other breakables that you wish to display, put them out of reach of children and pets.

Furniture as Storage—When purchasing furniture, consider storage possibilities. A trunk can serve as a coffee table and also hold extra blankets, photo albums, or games. You can buy end tables that have drawers, shelves, or even cabinets in them to store pens, paper, magazines, books, catalogs, or a box of tissues.

Silk Plants and Flowers—Flowers and greenery enliven a room. Use mostly silk plants and flowers because:

1. Silk plants don't need watering, fertilizing, trimming, or transplanting.

2. Silk plants don't turn brown and die; they always look good.

3. Pets don't eat the silk plants and then get sick on the carpet.

4. Silk plants are practically indestructible; they don't break if a ball hits them.

5. Silk plants are clean; if one gets knocked over, it's easier to clean up styrofoam and spanish moss than wet dirt.

6. Silk plants don't attract bugs or worms.

7. Silk plants can be ripped out by the roots, stuck in a sink full of soapy water, rinsed off, and air dried. Stick them back in their pots, and they look better than ever. In between baths, dust them with a feather duster.

Using What You Have—Search your cupboards for decorative dishes to hold candy, potpourri, candles, plants, or fruit. Plates can be hung on the wall or displayed on a shelf. Fill a glass canning jar with potpourri, beans, pasta, rice, candy, buttons, or cinnamon sticks, top it with a square of fabric or lace, and tie it with pretty ribbon.

Mat and frame posters, artwork, poetry, wedding invitations, greeting cards, or a beautiful magazine photo to hang on the wall. Frame snapshots to decorate an end table or bookshelf. Arrange handsome books between bookends to decorate a shelf. Make silk flowers from a wedding into a new arrangement or bouquet or use them to make a wreath or candle ring. Refurbish old wreaths with fresh vines and flowers. Use potpourri to cover the styrofoam in a potted silk plant (instead of spanish moss).

If you have a lace tablecloth that doesn't fit your table, use it on a dresser or sofa table. Fold it in half if need be, and place the folded edge at the back. Or drape it over a curtain rod as a loose curtain. Use large knots to hold it in place or tie it with ribbon. If the lace is torn or stained, cut it into pieces to use as doilies. Hang a quilt on the wall or toss it over the back of the sofa. For a really country look, use it as a tablecloth or fold it over an open cupboard door. Place a pretty hand towel on the toilet tank under a basket of bath products. Use cloth napkins, placemats, scarves, or handkerchiefs as doilies.

Look around you at what you have. Go through your closets, cupboards, and drawers. Use your imagination. Anything that's pretty or striking can be used to decorate. Check the basement, garage, or attic for fabulous forgotten finds. Don't forget to look outside. Transplant ivy or ferns from the woods. (Watch out for poison ivy.) Make fresh or dried flower bouquets, twig or grapevine wreaths, handsome stone bookends, or many other items from things found outside your doorstep.

Rearranging—There's often no need to buy new things for a fresh look. Rearrange the furniture. Be daring! Move the pictures, shelves, lamps, plants, curtains, throw pillows, candles, flower arrangements, and other decorative pieces from room to room. Bring a piece of porch furniture into the living room. Take the rocking chair into the bedroom. Set a large plant or floral arrangement in the fireplace for the summer, or use a collection of candles to provide a fire. Move things around!

Recover—When you can't replace, redo. Recovering upholstered furniture with slipcovers offers a less expensive solution to replacing the furniture. A pretty blanket, quilt, or afghan can also add a fresh touch, as would fresh throw pillows in various colors and patterns. Mix things up a little. Use a solid color slipcover on the sofa and a print on the chair or vice versa. Pull them together by using pillows of the opposite fabric (the chair's print on the solid sofa and the sofa's solid on the print chair). Throw in a coordinating check or plaid for additional pillows.

Paint—Paint gives a fresh look as well, for very little money. You need not repaint the entire room, although that's certainly an option. Paint a new color only below the chair rail or only above. Paint the woodwork, the ceiling, or the cabinets. Paint furniture in assorted brights or pastels. Stencil a border on the walls or an accent on a cupboard. Paint accessories or stencil lampshades. Use different paint techniques such as sponging, ragging, or marbling. (Practice on a picture frame or old board first.) Visit a craft store or paint store for ideas. Borrow books from the library for instructions on the technique. Be creative!

Daily Planner

The following pages may be photocopied for use in any daily planner. You may purchase a standard planner and add these pages, or you can use a simple notebook. No more searching for the perfect planner; customize this one to fit you. Photocopied pages can, of course, be altered any way you like. At the beginning of each year make fresh copies. Evaluate how you've grown and the accomplishments you've made. Photocopy the pages at the end of each chapter and add them to your planner to chart your progress. Use colored paper to color-code your planner by month, section, subject, or whatever method suits you. Add tabbed dividers to make things easier to find.

How to Use Your Planner

Monthly Page—Color-code this page or add a divider tab; there is one for each month of the year. The first nine months cover the fruit of the Spirit, and the year ends with seasonal subjects for the holidays.

Birthdays and Anniversaries—Photocopy this page onto the back of each monthly page. Fill in the birthdays and anniversaries at the beginning of the year. Fill in special occasions (weddings, baby showers, graduations) as they occur. At the beginning of each month, note those occasions you will need to plan for. Mark your shopping list for the cards and gifts you need to purchase.

Prayer Journal—Photocopy 12 of these pages, one for each month. This page should follow the birthday page and can also be color-coded. Each month, you may want to say a special prayer for those having birthdays. Many times we don't get around to praying for every friend, cousin, niece, nephew, aunt, and uncle. Pray for them during their birthday month! At the beginning of each month, fill in this page with confessions, praise, special petitions, and thanks. Try using the acronym CHAT: Confession, Honor, Ask, Thanks.

Month at a Glance—Photocopy this page onto the back of each prayer journal page. Fill in your goals for the month, and notes for any projects you plan to do. Use this page to plan your projects. Be sure to mark any supplies you need on your shopping list, and mark down errands necessary before you start your project.

Week at a Glance—Photocopy these two pages with the opposite page on the back. Tip: photocopy 52 Monday sides, then turn over and photocopy 52 weekend sides on the back. This two-page spread has a section at the top to remind you of goals for the week and includes space for meal planning. Because these pages are universal, the month and date will need to be filled in. It's best to complete these when you begin to use the planner. That way if you need to mark a date months in the future, you'll be able to do so quickly. Use a bold marker (that doesn't bleed through) so the dates will jump off the page at you. Using neon highlighter colors is not recommended because they tend to fade over time. After filling in all the dates, insert the color-coded monthly pages at the beginning of each month.

Shopping List—Insert the shopping list pages in the center of each week or if you prefer, color-code the shopping lists and keep them in the back. You can always remove the lists one at a time to insert in the current week. This saves some collating when putting your planner together. When planning the meals, jot down ingredients that need to be purchased. The grocery list is divided into sections for each main area of the store. This organizes your list to prevent running back three aisles because you missed something. This also prompts you to look at each section when making your list, and recall if you need things from a certain department. (You notice the health and beauty section is empty, and remember that you need to buy shampoo.) Remove this sheet to go shopping, but don't forget to run the errands marked on the back. Check to be sure everything on the list is taken care of before throwing it away. If something still needs to be done, either keep the list in your purse to do later or add it to next week's list.

Errands—Photocopy this page on the back of the shopping list. When using your planner to schedule a project, note the errands and supplies needed. When you're ready to run the errands, figure out the most efficient route to take care of them, and mark them one, two, three, and so forth on the list. The errands list is divided into two sections so you can remember what stops you need to make and what you need to buy or do at each one.

Gift Ideas—Use this page to record gift ideas you think of any time of the year. When a birthday or Christmas rolls around, look here for some great ideas. Record ideas for yourself too. When your husband wants to know what you'd like for Christmas, you'll be prepared—no more last-minute decisions!

Remember—Planning is essential to keep track of what is going on and what needs to be done. Planning also gives you boundaries between work and play. These boundaries afford you the discipline to get your work done, and allow you the freedom to enjoy your play without guilt. "But the noble man makes noble plans, and by noble deeds he stands" (Isaiah 32:8).

Commit to the LORD whatever you do, and
your plans will succeed. *Proverbs 16:3*

The LORD gives strength to His people;
the LORD blesses His people with
peace. *Psalm 29:11*

Happy New Year!

As we begin a fresh new year, let us celebrate the fruit of the Spirit, beginning with peace.

God's peace is the only true peace, a peace that "transcends all understanding" (Philippians 4:7). It's a peace that comes when we place everything—absolutely everything—into His hands; it's a peace that comes in the midst of utter despair; it's a peace that comes when the rest of the world is in utter chaos. Living in God's peace is a great way to start off the year!

"Peace I leave with you; My peace I give you. I do not give to you as the world gives. Do not let your hearts be troubled and do not be afraid." John 14:27

But the fruit of the Spirit is love, joy, peace, patience, kindness, goodness, faithfulness, gentleness, and self-control. *Galatians 5:22–23*

Feb

Happy Valentine's Day!

It's natural for this month's fruit of the Spirit to be love. Our most basic gift from God is love.

Dear friends, let us love one another, for love comes from God. Everyone who loves has been born of God and knows God. Whoever does not love does not know God, because God is love. This is how God showed His love among us: He sent His one and only Son into the world that we might live through Him. This is love: not that we loved God, but that He loved us and sent His Son as an atoning sacrifice for our sins. Dear friends, since God so loved us, we also ought to love one another. No one has ever seen God; but if we love one another, God lives in us and His love is made complete in us. *1 John 4:7–12*

How wonderful to be able to make God's love complete!

Be devoted to one another in brotherly love. Honor one another above yourselves. Romans 12:10

The wilderness will rejoice and blossom.
Like a crocus, it will burst into bloom;
it will rejoice greatly and shout for joy.
Isaiah 35:1–2

mar

The Easter season is approaching, and what a perfect time for it! All the plants of the earth bud and bloom and come back from the dead of winter. Appropriately, our fruit of the Spirit this month is joy. In Christ we find true joy, as we come back from the death of sin through Jesus' death and resurrection. "Yet I will rejoice in the Lord, I will be joyful in God my Savior" (Habakkuk 3:18).

May the God of hope fill you with all joy and peace as you trust in Him, so that you may over-flow with hope by the power of the Holy Spirit. Romans 15:13

And we pray this in order that you may live a life worthy of the Lord and may please Him in every way: bearing fruit in every good work, growing in the knowledge of God, being strengthened with all power according to His glorious might so that you may have great endurance and patience. *Colossians 1:10–11*

April

ur fruit of the Spirit this month is patience. April showers bring May flowers—be patient! Patience has been defined as the restraint of anger or resentment when opposed or oppressed. Patience is displayed not only with people, but with difficult circumstances as well. Remember Job? Despite all that happened to him, he declared, "As long as I have life within me, the breath of God in my nostrils, my lips will not speak wickedness, and my tongue will utter no deceit. I will never admit you are in the right; till I die, I will not deny my integrity. I will maintain my righteousness and never let go of it; my conscience will not reproach me as long as I live" (Job 27:3–6).

What was Job's reward for his loyalty and patience? "After Job had prayed for his friends, the LORD made him prosperous again and gave him twice as much as he had before. ... After this, Job lived a hundred and forty years; he saw his children and their children to the fourth generation" (Job 42:10, 16). May we all strive for the patience of Job.

A patient man has great understanding, but a quick-tempered man displays folly.
Proverbs 14:29

Be kind and compassionate to one
another, forgiving each other,
just as in Christ God forgave you.
Ephesians 4:32

May is here!

The flowers are blooming, the breezes are
warm, the earth is alive again! What a beautiful
symbol of Christ's resurrection! Our fruit of the
Spirit this month is kindness. "And the Lord's
servant must not quarrel; instead, he must be
kind to everyone, able to teach, not resentful.
Those who oppose him he must gently instruct,
in the hope that God will grant them repen-
tance leading them to a knowledge of the truth"
(2 Timothy 2:24–25).

*Always try to be kind to each
other and to everyone else.
1 Thessalonians 5:15*

I want you to be wise about what is
good, and innocent about what is evil.
Romans 16:19

June

A "fruit of the Spirit" is a trait shown
in us when our lives are given over to the Holy
Spirit. June's fruit of the Spirit is goodness. The
more Spirit-filled our lives are, the more goodness will be brought forth from us. When it
becomes difficult for us to "be good," we need to
yield to God's Holy Spirit. How do we do that?
First, pray; pray for God to fill our lives with
good until there's no room left for the bad. God
gives us a choice. We can fill our hearts with the
desires of our sinful nature, or we can fill them
with the fruit of His Holy Spirit. When the Spirit
lives in us, it shows! Jesus said, "The good man
brings good things out of the good stored up in
him, and the evil man brings evil things out of the
evil stored up in him" (Matthew 12:35).

Therefore, as we have opportunity,
let us do good to all people,
especially to those who belong
to the family of believers.

Galatians 6:10

So that your faith might not rest on men's wisdom, but on God's power.
1 Corinthians 2:5

Jaithfulness is our fruit of the Spirit for July. It would seem that every Christian is faithful. We have faith or we would not be Christians. However, being faithful means more than just believing. Are we faithful in our worship? In prayer? In reading God's Word? Are we faithful in our Christian example, even in the company of unbelievers? Are we faithful stewards of the gifts, talents, and blessings God has given us?

God is faithful to us, and even provides the means for us to be faithful to Him: "Faith comes from hearing the message, and the message is heard through the word of Christ" (Romans 10:17). May we all be able to say of this life, "I have fought the good fight, I have finished the race, I have kept the faith" (2 Timothy 4:7).

Love the LORD, all His saints! The LORD preserves the faithful. Psalm 31:23

Your beauty … should be that of your inner self, the unfading beauty of a gentle and quiet spirit, which is of great worth in God's sight. *1 Peter 3:3–4*

Aug

Gentleness is August's fruit of the Spirit. Gentleness is being kindly, not rough or violent, wellborn, easily handled or managed. Wellborn describes us exactly as the children of God! The King James Version of the Bible uses the word meekness in this verse. Meekness means being humbly patient, "spiritless," tame, gentle, or kind. *Spiritless*? Is this good? Think about it. The corresponding word is tame. A horse is referred to as "spirited" when it is wild and out of control; you can't do anything with it until that spirit is broken. Perhaps that is exactly how we are with God. He can't do anything with us until we submit to His Holy Spirit. Then we are tame, gentle, humble—meek. It is no longer our spirit at work, but God's. The more we are filled with His Spirit, the gentler we will be.

Be completely humble and gentle; be patient, bearing with one another in love. Ephesians 4:2

For the grace of God ... teaches us to say "No" to ungodliness and worldly passions and to live self-controlled, upright and godly lives in this present age. *Titus 2:11–12*

September's fruit of the Spirit is self-control—not a popular concept in today's society. Self-control is about doing what is right, good, and helpful, and avoiding what's wrong, harmful, and destructive. It's about saying no to excess food or drink, to sex outside of marriage, to spending money we don't have, to bad tempers, rage, and destructive use of our tongues—gossip, harsh words, bad language. It's also about saying yes to respectable, loving relationships, to spending time with family, to understanding and patience. Most of all, self-control is about living life as a reflection of Christ.

Like a city whose walls are broken down is a man who lacks self-control. Proverbs 25:28

Those who hope in the LORD will renew their strength. They will soar on wings like eagles; they will run and not grow weary, they will walk and not be faint. *Isaiah 40:31*

Oct

It is October already and the holiday season is fast approaching. As we anticipate busy days ahead, our focus this month will be strength. Trying to be everywhere, do it all, and do it all perfectly is not what God intends for the holidays, but far too often that's what becomes of them. With God's strength, we can avoid getting caught up in the hustle, bustle, and materialism of the holidays, and spend them as they're meant to be spent.

Plan now to remember what is truly important—giving our Lord thanks during the Thanksgiving holiday and celebrating His birth during the Christmas season. Praising God, worshiping, being together with our families, and loving one another are the keys to a fulfilling season; with the right focus and the strength of God, the coming months will be filled with peace.

Do not be dismayed, for I am your God. I will strengthen you and help you. Isaiah 41:10

Let us come before Him with thanksgiving and extol Him with music and song. *Psalm 95:2*

November's focus will be an "attitude of gratitude." Attitudes we carry with us can either make us happy and fulfilled or miserable and lonely. Normally, no one wants to be around someone "with an attitude," but a person with an "attitude of gratitude" is a joy to be around. No matter what happens, that person can find something to be glad about. No matter what life hands them, they resolve to make the best of any situation.

The apostle Paul was one of those people. In his letter to the Philippians, not only did he thank God for the church, but he also proclaimed near the end of the book that he had "learned to be content whatever the circumstances" (Philippians 4:11). Paul was in prison at the time. That is an attitude of gratitude! May we all follow Paul's example. Read the book of Philippians this month. (It's only four chapters.) It will inspire you!

And whatever you do, whether in word or deed, do it all in the name of the Lord Jesus, giving thanks to God the Father through Him. Colossians 3:17

Each one of you should use whatever gift he has received to serve others, faithfully administering God's grace in its various forms. *1 Peter 4:10*

During the Christmas season, the birth of our Savior is celebrated by the giving of gifts. While this custom may have begun with the Wise Men, the original giver was our heavenly Father, who gave us creation, salvation, and life itself. What better way to celebrate Christmas than to give something back to the One who gave so much for us? One way we can do that is to give back to God the special gifts and talents He has given us. Each one of us has many unique God-given abilities.

The best gift we can give is love, and sharing God's love is the best of all. What better time is there than Christmas? Christmas cards proclaiming His birth are one opportunity; even better is a personal witness of what Christ has done for you, or an invitation to worship with you. "But the angel said to them, 'Do not be afraid. I bring you good news of great joy that will be for all the people'" (Luke 2:10). You also are bringing good news of great joy! What a blessed gift to your loved one, what a blessed gift to God. Happy birthday, Jesus!

I remind you to fan into flame the gift of God, which is in you. ... For God did not give us a spirit of timidity, but a spirit of power. ... So do not be ashamed to testify about our Lord" (2 Timothy 1:6–9).

Happy Birthday

_____
_____
_____

_____
_____
_____

Happy Anniversary

_____
_____
_____

_____
_____
_____

Special Occasions

_____
_____
_____

_____

Prayer Journal

○

Confession—Lord, I confess and repent of my sins:

○

○

Honor—Lord, I honor and praise You for:

Ask—Lord, if it be Your will, please:

○

○

Thanks—Lork, I thank You for:

○

Month at a Glance

Goals for the month:

_____
_____
_____
_____
_____
_____
_____
_____

Project notes:

_____
_____
_____
_____
_____
_____
_____
_____

Week at a Glance

Goals for the week:

_____

_____

_____

Monday
Meals:

_____

_____

_____

_____

Tuesday
Meals:

_____

_____

_____

_____

Wednesday
Meals:

_____

_____

_____

Thursday
Meals:

_____

_____

_____

_____

Friday
Meals:

_____

_____

_____

_____

Saturday
Meals:

_____

_____

_____

_____

Sunday
Meals:

_____

_____

_____

_____

Shopping List

Produce

_____

_____

_____

Meat

_____

_____

_____

Dairy

_____

_____

_____

Frozen foods

_____

_____

_____

Baking goods

_____

_____

_____

Beverages

_____

_____

_____

_____

Cleaning supplies

_____

_____

_____

_____

Bakery

_____

_____

_____

Canned goods

_____

_____

_____

_____

Paper products

_____

_____

_____

_____

Health and beauty

_____

_____

_____

Other

_____

_____

_____

_____

_____

_____

_____

_____

_____

Errands

Stops to Make

To Buy or Do

Gift Ideas

Name _____

Birthday
_____

_____

Christmas _____

_____

Other
_____

Name _____

Birthday
_____

_____

Christmas _____

_____

Other
_____

Gift Ideas

Name _____

Birthday
_____

_____

Christmas
_____

_____

Other
_____

Name _____

Birthday
_____

_____

Christmas
_____

_____

Other
_____

Gift Ideas

Name _____

Birthday
_____

_____

Christmas
_____

_____

Other
_____

Name _____

Birthday
_____

_____

Christmas
_____

_____

Other
_____

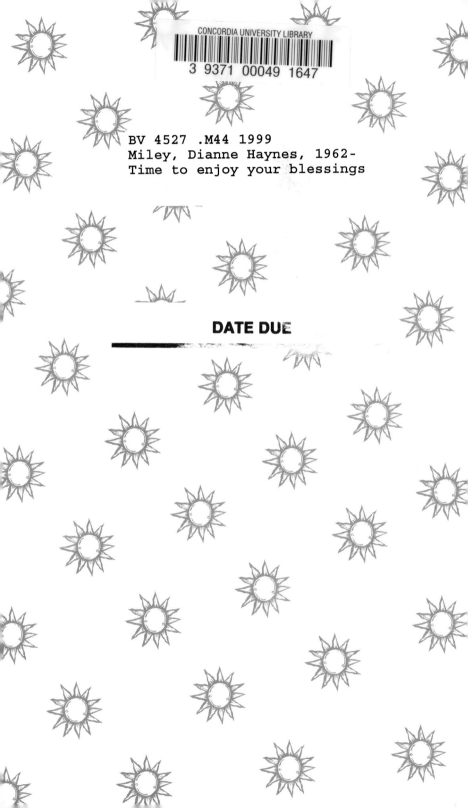